# FUN WITH CHINESE CHARACTERS

## The Straits Times Collection ③

Cartoonist: Tan Huay Peng

**FEDERAL PUBLICATIONS**
Singapore • Kuala Lumpur • Hong Kong

**Published for The Straits Times
by Federal Publications (S) Pte Ltd**

**© 1983 Federal Publications (S) Pte Ltd**
*A member of the Times Publishing Group*
Times Centre
1 New Industrial Road
Singapore 536196

First published 1983
Reprinted     1984, 1985, 1986, 1987 (twice),
              1988 (twice), 1989, 1990,
              1991 (twice), 1992 (twice), 1993,
              1994 (three times), 1995 (three times)

ISBN 981 01 3006 6

Printed by Chung Printing, Singapore

## PREFACE

**Fun With Chinese Characters Volume 3** features another 140 characters which first appeared in the Straits Times Bilingual Page. They trace systematically the evolution of Chinese characters from pictographs and ideographs, introducing radical elements and compounds with the appreciative and discerning eye of a cartoonist.

This final collection in the highly popular and successful Fun With Chinese Characters Series includes an indispensable index of all the characters found in the series for easy reference.

# CONTENTS 目录

| | | | | | | | | |
|---|---|---|---|---|---|---|---|---|
| 105 | 听 | tīng | 114 | 娘 | niáng | 123 | 石 | shí |
| 106 | 聋 | lóng | 115 | 妙 | miào | 124 | 仙 | xiān |
| 107 | 喜 | xǐ | 116 | 客 | kè | 125 | 高 | gāo |
| 108 | 春 | chūn | 117 | 比 | bǐ | 126 | 京 | jīng |
| 109 | 唱 | chàng | 118 | 背 | bèi | 127 | 空 | kōng |
| 110 | 歌 | gē | 119 | 凶 | xiōng | 128 | 船 | chuán |
| 111 | 鸣 | míng | 120 | 答 | dá | 129 | 贫 | pín |
| 112 | 吐 | tǔ | 121 | 篮 | lán | 130 | 圆 | yuán |
| 113 | 如 | rú | 122 | 井 | jǐng | 131 | 儿 | ér |

| | | |
|---|---|---|
| 132 | 士 | shì |
| 133 | 做 | zuò |
| 134 | 众 | zhòng |
| 135 | 价 | jià |
| 136 | 话 | huà |
| 137 | 语 | yǔ |
| 138 | 去 | qù |
| 139 | 回 | huí |
| 140 | 凸 | tū |
| | 凹 | āo |

**WÁNG**

king; ruler

THREE horizontal planes ( 三 ) representing heaven, man and earth, connected by a vertical structure ( 丨 ), form the character for king: 王 — the one vested with power, between heaven and earth, to rule uprightly over man. Originally 王 was a pictograph of a string of jade beads ( 王 ) which only the royalty could afford. It eventually became the symbol for king.

一 二 干 王 王

| | | | | |
|---|---|---|---|---|

| 国王 | guó wáng | king | 王宫 | wáng gōng | (imperial) palace |
|---|---|---|---|---|---|
| 王朝 | wáng cháo | imperial court; dynasty | 王牌 | wáng pái | trump card |
| 王储 | wáng chǔ | crown prince | 王室 | wáng shì | royal family; imperial court |
| 王法 | wáng fǎ | the law | 王位 | wáng wèi | throne |
| 王公贵族 | wáng gōng guì zú | the nobility | 王族 | wáng zú | persons of royal lineage |

*Example:*

国 王 死 后 ， 王 子 将 继 承 王 位 。
Guó wáng sǐ hòu　　wáng zi jiāng jì chéng wáng wèi
When the king dies, the prince will succeed to the throne.

1

# 玉

**YÙ**

jade; gem

三 represents 3 pieces of jade strung together as a symbol for king: 王. The dot (丶) was added to form 玉 (jade), distinguishing it from 王 (king). Highly valued as a symbol of excellence and purity, jade may be found in its crude form, hidden in rough stone. Hence the saying: "Jade which is not chiselled and polished is not an article of beauty."

一 二 干 王 玉 玉 玉

| 玉雕 | yù diāo | jade carving; jade sculpture |
| 玉皇大帝 | yù huáng dà dì | the Jade Emperor (the Supreme Deity of Taoism) |
| 玉洁冰清 | yù jié bīng qīng | as pure as jade and as clean as ice |
| 玉器 | yù qì | jade article |
| 玉色 | yù sè | jade green; light bluish green |
| 玉蜀黍 | yù shǔ shǔ | maize; corn |
| 玉兔 | yù tù | the Jade Hare — the moon |
| 玉簪 | yù zān | jade hairpin |

*Example:*

这 个 玉 雕 不 便 宜 。

Zhè ge yù diāo bù pián yi

This jade carving is not cheap.

2

# 国 (國)

**GUÓ**   country; nation

國 is composed of 囗 (boundary), 一 (land), 口 (mouth) and 戈 (spear). 國 therefore means land, people and weapons within a boundary — a country. The simplified form puts only 玉 (jade, representing king) within the boundary (囗) to produce nation: 国. But a king needs subjects as much as subjects need food: "People are the nation's source; food is the primary need of the people."

| 丨 | 冂 | 冂 | 冃 | 用 | 国 | 国 | 国 | 国 | 国 | | | | |

| | | | | | | | |
|---|---|---|---|---|---|---|---|
| 国宾 | guó bīn | state guest | | 国会 | guó huì | parliament |
| 国策 | guó cè | national policy | | 国籍 | guó jí | nationality |
| 国产 | guó chǎn | made in our country | | 国际 | guó jì | international |
| 国都 | guó dū | national capital | | 国内市场 | guó nèi shì chǎng | domestic market |
| 国法 | guó fǎ | the law of the land | | 国庆 | guó qìng | National Day |
| 国防 | guó fáng | national defence | | 国事访问 | guó shì fǎng wèn | state visit |
| 国歌 | guó gē | national anthem | | | | |

*Example:*

唱 国 歌 时 要 立 正 。

Chàng guó gē shi yào lì zhèng

Stand at attention when singing the national anthem.

3

# 现 （現）

**XIÀN**    appear; reveal; now

THE radical is 玉 (jade, gem) contracted to 王. The phonetic 見, representing eyes (目) of man (儿), means to see. So 現 means the sight of a sparkling gem, its appearance at that very moment; now. Appearances may be revealing or deceptive. According to the saying: "Fine words and appearance are seldom associated with virtue."

| 一 | 二 | 千 | 王 | 扫 | 玑 | 现 | 现 | | | | | |

| | | | | | |
|---|---|---|---|---|---|
| 现场 | xiàn chǎng | scene (of an incident) | 现象 | xiàn xiàng | appearance (of things); phenomenon |
| 现成 | xiàn chéng | ready-made | | | |
| 现代 | xiàn dài | modern times; the contemporary age | 现有 | xiàn yǒu | now available; existing |
| | | | 现在 | xiàn zài | now; at present; today |
| 现款 | xiàn kuǎn | ready money; cash | 出现 | chū xiàn | appear |
| 现实 | xiàn shí | reality; actuality | 发现 | fā xiàn | discover |

*Example:*

她 脸 上 现 出 一 丝 笑 容 。

Tā liǎn shàng xiàn chū yī sī xiào róng

A faint smile appeared on her face.

4

**里**

**LǏ** village; mile; inside

里 originally was a village made up of 田 (fields) and 土 (earth). The average length of one side, about 600 metres, became a measure of length: 里 , a Chinese mile. 里 is also the simplified form of 裏 . Here the radical for clothes (衣) is split and lined inside with the phonetic 里 to suggest inside: 裏 .

丶 冂 冃 日 旦 甲 里 里 里

| 里边 | lǐ bian | inside; in; within |
| 里程 | lǐ chéng | mileage; course of development |
| 里程碑 | lǐ chéng bēi | milestone |
| 里海 | Lǐ Hǎi | the Caspian Sea |
| 里面 | lǐ miàn | inside; interior |
| 里头 | lǐ tou | inside; interior |

*Example:*

屋 子 里 面 充 满 阳 光 。
Wū zi lǐ miàn chōng mǎn yáng guāng
The house is filled with sunshine.

## 理 LǏ

polish;
reason;
principle

玉 (gem) is the radical, and the phonetic 里 is made up of 田 (field) and 土 (land). 理 compares the cutting of a gem to the dividing of field and land, both done according to fixed rules and principles; hence the extended meaning: reason, principle. The old saying highlights the importance of a moral standard: "A man of talent without principle is inferior to a simpleton with principle."

一 二 干 王 玎 玑 玥 珇 珇 理 理

| 理睬 | lǐ cǎi | (usually in the negative) pay attention to; show interest in |
| 理发 | lǐ fà | haircut; hairdressing |
| 理会 | lǐ huì | understand; comprehend |
| 理解 | lǐ jiě | understand; comprehend |
| 理科 | lǐ kē | science (as a school subject) |

| 理论 | lǐ lùn | theory |
| 理事会 | lǐ shì huì | council; board of directors |
| 理所当然 | lǐ suǒ dāng rán | of course; naturally |
| 理想 | lǐ xiǎng | ideal |
| 理性 | lǐ xìng | reason |
| 理由 | lǐ yóu | reason; ground; argument |
| 理智 | lǐ zhì | reason; intellect |

*Example:*

我 有 充 分 理 由 相 信 他 的 话 。
Wǒ yǒu chōng fèn lǐ yóu xiāng xìn tā de huà

I have every reason to believe his words.

**ZHǓ**   owner; master

主 **is a pictograph of a lampstand with the flame rising above it. It symbolises a man who spreads light — a lord or master. To shed light, the master himself needs the enlightening counsel: "If you suspect a man, don't employ him; if you employ a man, don't suspect him."**

丶 一 二 主 主

| | | | |
|---|---|---|---|
| 主办 | zhǔ bàn | direct; sponsor | |
| 主持 | zhǔ chí | chair (a discussion); host (a banquet) | |
| 主动 | zhǔ dòng | initiative | |
| 主队 | zhǔ duì | home team; host team | |
| 主妇 | zhǔ fù | housewife; hostess | |
| 主观 | zhǔ guān | subjective | |
| 主管 | zhǔ guǎn | person in charge | |

| | | |
|---|---|---|
| 主人 | zhǔ rén | master |
| 主任 | zhǔ rèn | director; chairman |
| 主使 | zhǔ shǐ | instigate; incite; abet |
| 主题 | zhǔ tí | theme; subject; motif |
| 主席 | zhǔ xí | chairman (of a meeting) |
| 主要 | zhǔ yào | main; chief; principal |
| 主义 | zhǔ yì | doctrine; -ism |
| 主意 | zhǔ yì | idea; plan; decision |

*Example:*

我 们 应 该 主 动 去 接 近 他 。
Wǒ men yīng gāi zhǔ dòng qù jiē jìn tā
We ought to take the initiative to befriend him.

# 住

**ZHÙ**

live;
reside;
stay

人 (man) is combined with 主 (master) to form 住, meaning to dwell. In ancient days, the man (人) was always master (主) of his dwelling; so the combination 住 suggests to dwell, to stay. In modern times, however, some husbands still boss the house; others house the boss.

ノ 亻 亻 亻 仁 住 住

| | | | | | |
|---|---|---|---|---|---|

住户　　zhù hù　　　household; resident
住口　　zhù kǒu　　shut up; stop talking
住手　　zhù shǒu　　stay one's hand; stop
住宿　　zhù sù　　　stay; put up; get accommodation
住院　　zhù yuàn　　be in hospital; be hospitalized
住宅　　zhù zhái　　residence; dwelling

*Example:*

他 大 部 分 时 间 在 学 校 住 宿 。
Tā dà bù fèn shí jiān zài xué xiào zhù sù
He stayed at the school most of the time.

8

## 全

**QUÁN**

complete;
perfect

THIS character was first written 全 or 全, combining 亼 (joined) with 工 (work). It means completed, i.e., the components are assembled and the work finished. However, the modern character, classified under 入 (in), could be interpreted as a jade (王 or 玉) skilfully inlaid (入), and so flawless and perfect: 全. But perfection is not always the crucial thing: "Better an imperfect jade than a perfect tile."

| 丿 | 人 | 亼 | 合 | 全 | 全 | | | | | | | | |

| | | | | | | |
|---|---|---|---|---|---|---|
| 全部 | quán bù | whole; complete; total; all | 全局 | quán jú | overall situation |
| 全才 | quán cái | a versatile person; all-rounder | 全力 | quán lì | with all one's strength |
| 全场 | quán chǎng | the whole audience; all those present | 全面 | quán miàn | overall; comprehensive |
| | | | 全年 | quán nián | annual; yearly |
| 全国性 | quán guó xìng | nationwide | 全球 | quán qiú | the whole world |
| 全集 | quán jí | complete works; collected works | 全套 | quán tào | complete set |
| 全景 | quán jǐng | panorama; full view | | | |

*Example:*

我 们 全 家 人 出 去 了 。

Wǒ men quán jiā rén chū qu le

My family had gone out.

9

# 痊

**QUÁN**     recover from illness

THE radical 疒 (originally 疒 )
represents a sick patient lying down
( 一 ) on a bed ( 爿 ). The phonetic 全
means finished or completed. The
combination 痊 is based on the belief
of physicians that when a disease
( 疒 ) has run its full course ( 全 ), the
patient recovers: 痊 .

| 、 | 二 | 广 | 广 | 疒 | 疒 | 疒 | 疢 | 疹 | 痊 | 痊 | | | |
|---|---|---|---|---|---|---|---|---|---|---|---|---|---|

痊愈     quán yù     fully recover from an illness

*Example:*

他 的 病 还 没 有 完 全 痊 愈 。
Tā  de  bìng  hái  méi  yǒu  wán  quán  quán  yù
He has not fully recovered from his illness.

10

**MǏ**

rice
(uncooked)

米 is a pictograph of a rice stalk. Its original form depicted nine grains of rice ⁘. This was modified to 米 and finally 米, symbolising grains (⼂) separated in the four quarters (十) by threshing. Although the rice-bowl may represent an honest means of living, "rice obtained by crookedness will not boil up into good food."

| 丶 | 丷 | 丷 | 半 | 米 | 米 | | | | | | | | | | |
|---|---|---|---|---|---|---|---|---|---|---|---|---|---|---|---|

| 米波 | mǐ bō | metric wave |
|---|---|---|
| 米粉 | mǐ fěn | rice-flour noodles; vermicelli |
| 米酒 | mǐ jiǔ | rice wine |
| 米粒 | mǐ lì | grain of rice |
| 米色 | mǐ sè | cream-coloured |
| 米制 | mǐ zhì | the metric system |

*Example:*

这 米 煮 得 太 烂 了 。

Zhè mǐ zhǔ de tài làn le

This rice is overcooked.

**FĚN**

powder

FACE powder in China was once made by grinding rice into fine particles. Hence the ideograph: 粉 meaning face powder — from 米 (rice) and 分 (divide, grind). The radical 米 is a likeness of a rice stalk and the phonetic 分 is a picture of a knife severing an object. 粉 now stands for anything ground into powder.

丶 丷 ⺌ ⺵ ⺼ 米 米 粉 粉 粉

| 粉笔 | fěn bǐ | chalk |
|------|--------|-------|
| 粉刺 | fěn cì | acne |
| 粉红 | fěn hóng | pink |
| 粉身碎骨 | fěn shēn suì gǔ | have one's body smashed to pieces; die the most cruel death |
| 粉刷 | fěn shuā | whitewash |
| 粉丝 | fěn sī | vermicelli made from bean starch, etc. |
| 粉碎 | fěn suì | smash; shatter; crush |

*Example:*

他 把 米 磨 成 粉 。

Tā bǎ mǐ mó chéng fěn

He grinds the rice into powder form.

12

# 精

**JĪNG**  refined; essence; vigour

米 (rice) is the radical of this character and 青 (green, pure) the phonetic. Rice, the only grain that grows in a padi field, is never mixed with other grains, and so signifies something pure. 青 (green) is also a symbol of purity; it is the colour of vegetation, 丹 representing the alchemist's stove and 生 the growing plant. The two symbols of purity combine to enforce the idea of refinement, essence or vigour: 米青.

丶 丷 ⼎ ⺜ ⺧ 半 米 米 粐 粐 粨 精 精 精

| 精兵 | jīng bīng | picked troops; crack troops |
| 精彩 | jīng cǎi | brilliant; splendid; wonderful |
| 精力 | jīng lì | energy; vigour |
| 精美 | jīng měi | exquisite; elegant |
| 精明强干 | jīng míng qiáng gàn | capable; able and efficient |
| 精疲力竭 | jīng pí lì jié | exhausted; worn out |

| 精巧 | jīng qiǎo | exquisite; ingenious |
| 精神 | jīng shén | spirit; mind; vigour; drive |
| 精心 | jīng xīn | meticulously; elaborately |
| 精液 | jīng yè | seminal fluid; semen |
| 精制 | jīng zhì | made with extra care |
| 精致 | jīng zhì | fine; exquisite |

*Example:*

这 花 瓶 的 雕 刻 很 精 致 。
Zhè huā píng de diāo kè hěn jīng zhì
The carvings on this vase are exquisite.

13

# 气（氣）

**Qì**  breath; vapour; air

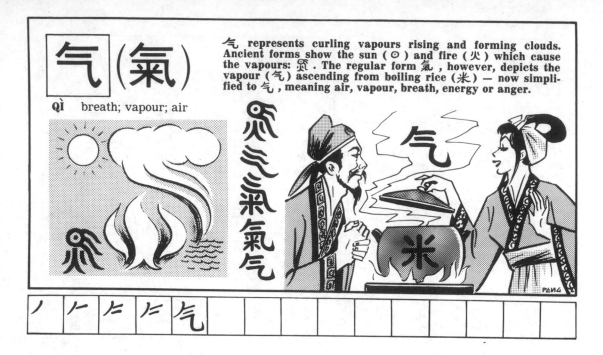

气 represents curling vapours rising and forming clouds. Ancient forms show the sun (☉) and fire (火) which cause the vapours: 氕. The regular form 氣, however, depicts the vapour (气) ascending from boiling rice (米) — now simplified to 气, meaning air, vapour, breath, energy or anger.

| | | | | |
|---|---|---|---|---|
| 丿 | 丿 | 二 | 二 | 气 |

| 气冲冲 | qì chōng chōng | furious; beside oneself with rage | 气候 | qì hòu | climate |
|---|---|---|---|---|---|
| 气喘 | qì chuǎn | asthma | 气力 | qì lì | effort; energy; strength |
| 气氛 | qì fēn | atmosphere | 气球 | qì qiú | balloon |
| 气愤 | qì fèn | indignant; furious | 气温 | qì wēn | air temperature |
| | | | 气象台 | qì xiàng tái | meteorological observatory |

*Example:*

会 谈 在 亲 切 友 好 的 气 氛 中 进 行 。
Huì tán zài qīng qiè yǒu hǎo de qì fēn zhōng jìn xíng
The talks were held in a cordial and friendly atmosphere.

14

**SHÍ**     eat; food

食, to eat, is the radical relating to food in general. Its seal form shows that it is made up of 亼 (together) and 皀 (boiled grain, food). 皀 itself is a pictograph of the rice-pot ( ㅂ ) and its contents ( – ) with a spoon or ladle ( ヒ ). 食 is the signal to come together ( 亼 ) to eat the food ( 皀 ). But food, like knowledge, needs to be properly digested. So: "Be quick over your work, but not over your food."

| 丿 | 人 | 亽 | 今 | 今 | 今 | 食 | 食 | 食 | | | | | | |

| | | | |
|---|---|---|---|
| 月食 | yuè shí | lunar eclipse | |
| 主食 | zhǔ shí | staple food | |
| 食粮 | shí liáng | grain; food | |
| 食品 | shí pǐn | foodstuff; food; provisions | |
| 食谱 | shí pǔ | recipes; cookbook | |

| | | |
|---|---|---|
| 食宿 | shí sù | board and lodging |
| 食堂 | shí táng | dining room; mess hall; canteen |
| 食物 | shí wù | food; eatables; edibles |
| 食言 | shí yán | go back on one's word; break one's promise |
| 食指 | shí zhǐ | index finger |

*Example:*

米 是 亚 洲 人 的 主 食 。
Mǐ shì Yà zhōu rén de zhǔ shì
Rice is the staple food of Asians.

# 饭（飯）

**FÀN**  rice (cooked)

飯, the character for cooked rice, comes from the radical 食 (food) and the phonetic 反 meaning return. 反 represents the repetitive motion (丆) of the hand (又), as in eating (食). Although hungry people are not fastidious about food, "One speck of rat's dung spoils a whole pot of rice." In combination, 食 is simplified to 饣.

丿　勹　饣　饣　饣　饭　饭

| | | | |
|---|---|---|---|
| 饭菜 | fàn cài | meal; repast |
| 饭店 | fàn diàn | restaurant |
| 饭锅 | fàn guō | pot for cooking rice; rice cooker |
| 饭桶 | fàn tǒng | rice bucket; big eater; good-for-nothing |
| 饭碗 | fàn wǎn | rice bowl; job; means of livelihood |
| 饭桌 | fàn zhuō | dining table |

*Example:*

这 餐 厅 饭 菜 可 口 ， 服 务 又 周 到 。
Zhè cān tīng fàn cài kě kǒu　fú wù yòu zhōu dào
This restaurant offers tasty food and good service.

16

**BĂO** eat to the full

包 the phonetic combines with 食, the radical for food, to form 飽 (satiated). The seal form of 包 is 包, depicting a foetus enclosed in the body; hence the meaning wrapped up. 飽 therefore means food all wrapped up in the stomach, i.e., fully satisfied. However, as the saying goes: "Better be hungry and pure than well-filled and corrupt."

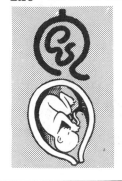

| 饱含 | bǎo hán | filled with |
| 饱和 | bǎo hé | saturation |
| 饱满 | bǎo mǎn | full; plump |
| 饱学 | bǎo xué | learned |

*Example:*

她 的 眼 睛 饱 含 着 幸 福 的 热 泪 。
Tā  de  yǎn jīng bǎo hán zhe xìng fú  de  rè  lèi

Her eyes were filled with tears of joy.

**È hungry**

THIS character is based on the radical for food: 食. It literally means feed (食) me (我) — a fitting sign for hunger. Another character for hunger is 饑, literally: little (幾) food (食), simplified to 饥, i.e., food (饣) on small table (几). Although hunger is no respecter of persons, "Even a hungry person will refuse food offered in contempt."

| ノ | 勺 | 勺 | 饣 | 饣 | 饣 | 饣 | 伴 | 饿 | 饿 |  |  |  |  |

| 挨饿 | āi è | go hungry |
| 饥饿 | jī è | hunger; starvation |
| 饿虎扑食 | è hǔ pū shí | like a hungry tiger pouncing on its prey |

*Example:*

他 挣 扎 在 饥 饿 线 上 。
Tā zhēng zhá zài jī è xiàn shang
She struggled along on the verge of death.

**GUǍN** hotel; restaurant

THE food radical 食 combines with 官 to produce 館, a public building. The phonetic 官 (official) originally meant the residence of an official — the hall (宀) of the city (㠯). 食 (food) together with 官 suggests a public building doing food business — inn, hotel or restaurant. Hence: "An innkeeper never worries if your appetite is big."

| 丿 | 𠃌 | 饣 | 𰯂 | 饣 | 饣 | 饣 | 饣 | 饣 | 馆 | 馆 | | | |

| 旅馆 | lǚ guǎn | hotel |
| 美术馆 | měi shù guǎn | art gallery |
| 体育馆 | tǐ yù guǎn | gymnasium; stadium |
| 图书馆 | tú shū guǎn | library |

*Example:*

这 旅 馆 的 布 置 很 堂 皇 。
Zhè lǚ guǎn de bù zhì hěn táng huáng
The hotel's decor is very impressive.

# 饮 (飲)

**YǏN**    drink

BASED on the food radical 食, this character has a significant phonetic 欠, suggesting breath. 欠 originally was a pictograph of a man opening his mouth to catch his breath, as in drinking: 欠. This was modified to 欠, representing air waves ( 彡 ) emanating from the man ( 儿 ). The primitive form of the character for drink shows clearly a drinking flask ( 酉 ) as part of the food radical.

丿 ⺈ 乞 钅 饣 饮 饮

| 饮茶 | yǐn chá | drink tea |
| 饮弹 | yǐn dàn | be hit by a bullet |
| 饮恨 | yǐn hèn | nurse a grievance |
| 饮料 | yǐn liào | drink; beverage |
| 饮泣 | yǐn qì | weep in silence |
| 饮食 | yǐn shí | food and drink; diet |
| 饮用水 | yǐn yòng shuǐ | drinking water; potable water |

*Example:*

他 喜 欢 早 上 在 茶 楼 饮 茶 。
Tā xǐ huān zǎo shang zài chá lóu yǐn chá
He likes to drink tea at the teahouse in the morning.

20

# 车 (車)

**CHĒ**
cart;
carriage;
chariot

車 represents a bird's eye view of a cart, showing its body ( 日 ), the two wheels ( 二 ) and the axle ( │ ). The primitive forms of 車 are as varied as carts, carriages and chariots. But, whatever the form, where there is a cart in front there is a track behind; so "Take warning from the wrecked cart ahead of you."

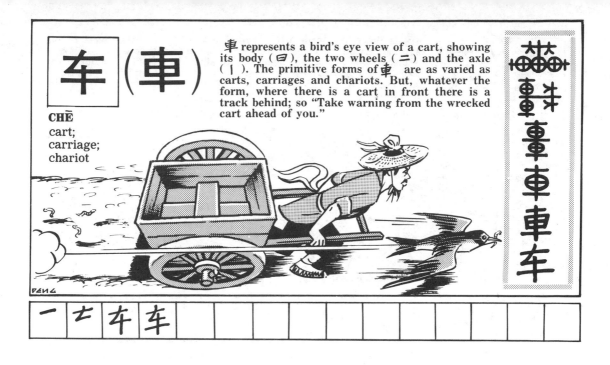

| 一 | 𠃋 | 车 | 车 | | | | | | | | | | | | |
|---|---|---|---|---|---|---|---|---|---|---|---|---|---|---|---|

| | | | | | | |
|---|---|---|---|---|---|---|
| 汽车 | qì chē | motor vehicle; automobile | | 车轮 | chē lún | wheel (of a vehicle) |
| 车床 | chē chuáng | lathe | | 车票 | chē piào | train or bus ticket |
| 车费 | chē fèi | fare | | 车水马龙 | chē shuǐ mǎ lóng | heavy traffic |
| 车祸 | chē huò | road accident | | 车速 | chē sù | speed of a motor vehicle |
| 车间 | chē jiān | workshop | | 车胎 | chē tāi | tyre |
| 车辆 | chē liàng | vehicle; car | | 车站 | chē zhàn | station; depot; stop |

*Example:*

这 条 街 的 汽 车 真 多 。
Zhè tiáo jiē de qì chē zhēn duō
This street is full of vehicles.

21

轰 (轟) is the triple form of the noisy cart (車). It serves as a fitting symbol for any loud or explosive sound like the rumbling of many carts. In the simplified form, 又 (again; ditto) replaces each of the two lower carts to produce 轰. 又 itself is a simplified picture of the right hand; and the right hand, returning repeatedly to the mouth in eating, suggests "again".

**HŌNG**   bang; boom (noise; uproar)

| 一 | 七 | 车 | 车 | 轱 | 轱 | 轰 | 轰 | | | | | | |
|---|---|---|---|---|---|---|---|---|---|---|---|---|---|

| | | |
|---|---|---|
| 轰动 | hōng dòng | cause a sensation; make a stir |
| 轰轰烈烈 | hōng hōng liè liè | on a grand and spectacular scale; vigorous; dynamic |
| 轰击 | hōng jī | shell; bombard |
| 轰隆 | hōng lōng | rumble; roll |
| 轰鸣 | hōng míng | thunder; roar |
| 轰炸 | hōng zhà | bomb |

*Example:*

她 的 超 级 迷 你 裙 使 全 场 轰 动 起 来 。

Tā  de  chāo jí  mí  ni  qún  shǐ  quán chǎng hōng dòng qǐ  lái

Her ultra-miniskirt caused a stir at the party.

22

# 库 (庫)

**KÙ**    storehouse

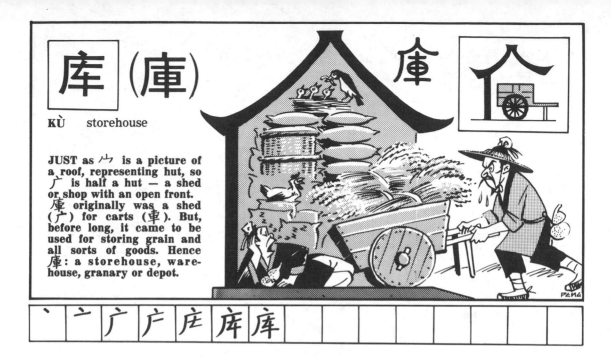

JUST as 宀 is a picture of a roof, representing hut, so 广 is half a hut — a shed or shop with an open front. 庫 originally was a shed (广) for carts (車). But, before long, it came to be used for storing grain and all sorts of goods. Hence 庫: a storehouse, warehouse, granary or depot.

丶   亠   广   庐   庄   库   库

| | | |
|---|---|---|
| 军械库 | jūn xiè kù | armoury |
| 仓库 | cāng kù | storehouse; warehouse |
| 库藏 | kù cáng | have in storage |
| 库存 | kù cún | stock; reserve |
| 库房 | kù fáng | storehouse |

*Example:*

这 仓 库 可 以 容 纳 大 量 货 物 。
Zhè cāng kù kě yǐ róng nà dà liàng huò wù
This warehouse can accomodate a large amount of goods.

23

# 轮 (輪)

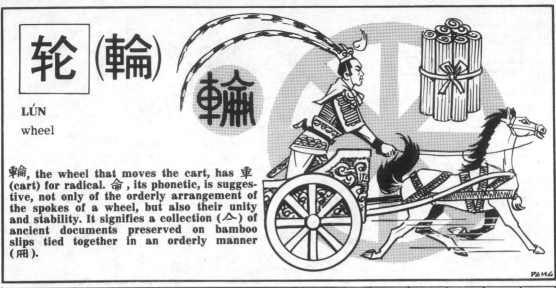

**LÚN**

wheel

輪, the wheel that moves the cart, has 車 (cart) for radical. 侖, its phonetic, is suggestive, not only of the orderly arrangement of the spokes of a wheel, but also their unity and stability. It signifies a collection (亼) of ancient documents preserved on bamboo slips tied together in an orderly manner (冊).

一 圡 车 车 轮 轮 轮 轮

| | | | |
|---|---|---|---|
| 轮班 | lún bān | in shifts; in relays | |
| 轮齿 | lún chǐ | teeth of a cogwheel | |
| 轮船 | lún chuán | steamer | |
| 轮渡 | lún dù | ferry | |
| 轮换 | lún huàn | rotate; take turns | |
| 轮机 | lún jī | turbine | |
| 轮廓 | lún kuò | outline; contour; rough sketch | |
| 轮流 | lún liú | take turns; do something in turn | |
| 轮胎 | lún tāi | tyre | |
| 轮椅 | lún yǐ | wheelchair | |
| 轮轴 | lún zhóu | wheel and axle | |
| 轮子 | lún zi | wheel | |

*Example:*

这 个 车 轮 被 刮 坏 了 。
Zhè ge chē lún bèi guā huài le

The wheel of this car was badly scratched.

# 军 (軍)

**JŪN** army; soldiers

THE seal form of this character shows a war chariot (車) escorted by a surrounding force of soldiers (勹) — an army: 軍. Armies are maintained for years, to be used on a single day. And on that crucial day: "The conquerors are crowned kings; the defeated are branded bandits."

丶 丶冖 冖 冒 军 军 军

| | | | |
|---|---|---|---|
| 军备 | jūn bèi | armament; arms | |
| 军部 | jūn bù | army headquarters | |
| 军操 | jūn cāo | military drill | |
| 军车 | jūn chē | military vehicle | |
| 军队 | jūn duì | armed forces | |
| 军法 | jūn fǎ | military criminal code | |
| 军港 | jūn gǎng | naval port | |
| 军官 | jūn guān | officer | |

| | | |
|---|---|---|
| 军火 | jūn huǒ | arms and ammunition |
| 军力 | jūn lì | military strength |
| 军人 | jūn rén | soldier; serviceman |
| 军士 | jūn shì | noncommissioned officer (NCO) |
| 军事训练 | jūn shì xùn liàn | military training |
| 军事演习 | jūn shì yǎn xí | military manoeuvre; war exercise |
| 军营 | jūn yíng | military camp; barracks |

*Example:*

军 人 的 工 作 是 很 有 挑 战 性 的 。
Jūn rén de gōng zuò shi hěn yǒu tiǎo zhàn xìng de
The work of a soldier is full of challenges.

25

# 斩 (斬)

**ZHǍN**    chop off

斬 probably has reference to a war chariot (車) with warriors wielding axes (斤) to cut off the enemy. It may also mean to whirl or brandish (車) a battle axe (斤). But cutting off an enemy does not eradicate the source of trouble; hence the saying: "When cutting the weeds, get rid of the root" (斩草除根).

| 一 | 土 | 车 | 车 | 车′ | 斩 | 斩 | 斩 | | | | | | |
|---|---|---|---|---|---|---|---|---|---|---|---|---|---|

斩草除根    zhǎn cǎo chú gēn    destroy root and branch — stamp out the source of trouble
斩钉截铁    zhǎn dīng jié tiě    resolute and decisive; categorical
斩断    zhǎn duàn    chop off
斩首    zhǎn shǒu    behead; decapitate

*Example:*

他 的 手 被 机 器 斩 断 了 。
Tā  de  shǒu bèi  jī  qì  zhǎn duàn le
His hands were chopped off by the machine.

26

# 轿 (轎)

**JIÀO**   sedan-chair

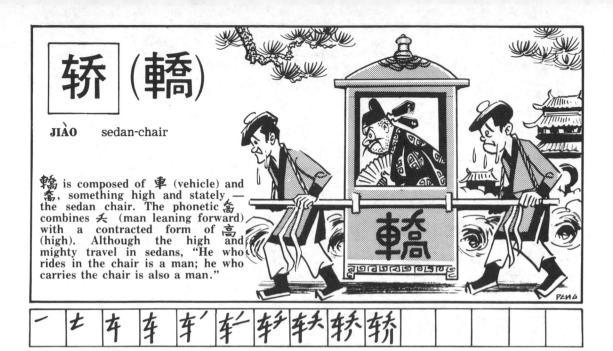

轎 is composed of 車 (vehicle) and 喬, something high and stately — the sedan chair. The phonetic 喬 combines 夭 (man leaning forward) with a contracted form of 高 (high). Although the high and mighty travel in sedans, "He who rides in the chair is a man; he who carries the chair is also a man."

一 十 车 车 车′ 车⁻ 轺 轶 轿 轿

| | | | |
|---|---|---|---|
| 轿车 | jiào chē | car |
| 轿子 | jiào zi | sedan chair |
| 花轿 | huā jiào | bridal sedan chair |

*Example:*

古 时 候 的 华 人 新 娘 是 坐 花 轿 的 。

Gǔ shí huò de huá rén xīn niáng shi zuò huā jiào de

In the olden days, Chinese brides rode on bridal sedan chairs.

27

# 软 (軟)

**RUǍN**

soft; weak;
pliable
yielding;

THE mobility of the carriage (車) is used to good effect in this character. Combined with 欠, it produces 軟, meaning soft and weak or pliable and flexible, 欠 signifying a man (儿) gasping for breath (彡), i.e., exhausted, deficient. 軟 may also be written 輭, the phonetic 耎 representing the soft beard (而) of a man (大).

一 十 车 车 车 轵 软 软

| 软钢 | ruǎn gāng | mild steel; soft steel |
| 软骨头 | ruǎn gú tou | a weak-kneed person; a spineless person; a coward |
| 软骨 | ruǎn gǔ | cartilage |
| 软化 | ruǎn huà | soften; win over by soft tactics |
| 软和 | ruǎn huo | gentle; kind; soft |
| 软件 | ruǎn jiàn | software |
| 软禁 | ruǎn jìn | put somebody under house arrest |
| 软弱 | ruǎn ruò | weak; feeble; flabby |

*Example:*

她 被 他 的 甜 言 蜜 语 软 化 了 。
Tā bèi tā de tián yán mì yǔ ruǎn huà le
She was won over by his sweet words.

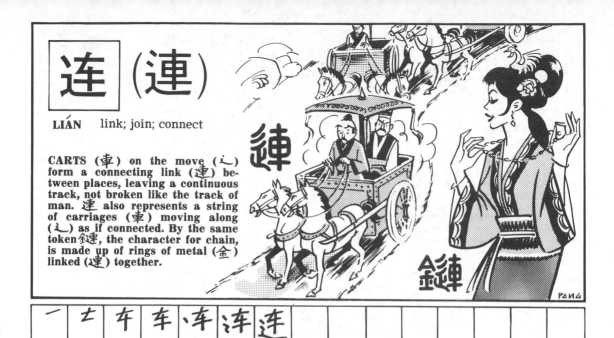

# 连 (連)

**LIÁN**　link; join; connect

CARTS (車) on the move (辶) form a connecting link (連) between places, leaving a continuous track, not broken like the track of man. 連 also represents a string of carriages (車) moving along (辶) as if connected. By the same token 鏈, the character for chain, is made up of rings of metal (金) linked (連) together.

| 一 | 士 | 车 | 车 | 车 | 车 | 浐 | 连 | | | | | | |
|---|---|---|---|---|---|---|---|---|---|---|---|---|---|

| 连贯 | lián guàn | link up; piece together; hang together; coherent; consistent |
|---|---|---|
| 连环画 | lián huán huà | a book (usually for children) with a story told in pictures; picture story book |
| 连累 | lián lěi | implicate; involve; get somebody into trouble |
| 连忙 | lián máng | promptly; at once |
| 连日 | lián rì | for days on end; day after day |
| 连同 | lián tóng | together with; along with |
| 连续 | lián xù | continuous; successive |
| 连夜 | lián yè | the same night; that very night |

*Example:*

小 梅 喜 欢 看 香 港 的 连 续 剧 。
Xiǎo méi xǐ huān kàn Xiāng Gǎng de lián xù jù
Xiaomei likes to watch the Hongkong serialised dramas.

# 莲（蓮）

**LIÁN** lotus

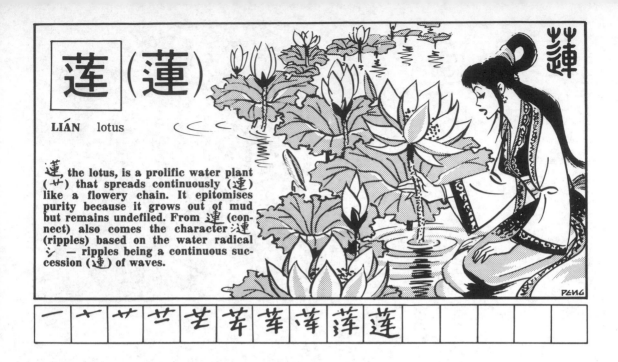

蓮 the lotus, is a prolific water plant (艹) that spreads continuously (連) like a flowery chain. It epitomises purity because it grows out of mud but remains undefiled. From 連 (connect) also comes the character 漣 (ripples) based on the water radical 氵 — ripples being a continuous succession (連) of waves.

一 十 卄 艹 芒 芒 芏 茊 茊 莲

| 莲花 | lián huā | lotus flower |
| 莲蓬 | lián peng | seedpod of the lotus |
| 莲蓬头 | lián peng tóu | shower nozzle |
| 莲子 | lián zǐ | lotus seed |

*Example:*

莲 花 是 生 长 在 水 里 的 。
Lián huā  shì shēng zhǎng zài shuǐ lǐ  de
Lotus flowers grow in water.

**FÙ**

父

father

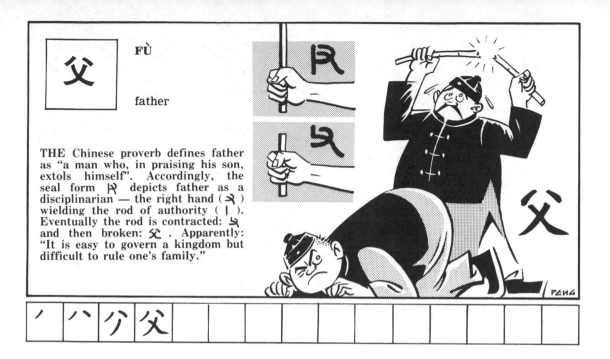

THE Chinese proverb defines father as "a man who, in praising his son, extols himself". Accordingly, the seal form 𢻰 depicts father as a disciplinarian — the right hand ( 𦥑 ) wielding the rod of authority ( | ). Eventually the rod is contracted: 𢼸 and then broken: 父 . Apparently: "It is easy to govern a kingdom but difficult to rule one's family."

ノ 八 分 父

| 父母 | fù mǔ | father and mother; parents |
| 父亲 | fù qin | father |
| 父权制 | fù quán zhì | patriarchy |
| 父兄 | fù xiōng | father and elder brothers; head of a family |

*Example:*

我 的 父 亲 是 个 慈 祥 的 人 。

Wǒ de fù qin shì ge cí xiáng de rén

My father is a kindly person.

31

## JĪN

巾

napkin; towel; handkerchief

巾 is a pictograph of a small piece of cloth used for cleaning, dusting or wiping. In ancient times it was worn, suspended from the girdle. 冂 represents the two extremities of the cloth hanging ( | ) from the girdle. 巾 forms the radical of a series of characters relating to cloth in general.

| 丨 | 冂 | 巾 | | | | | | | | | | | |
|---|---|---|---|---|---|---|---|---|---|---|---|---|---|

| 巾帼 | jīn guó | woman |
|---|---|---|
| 巾帼英雄 | jīn guó yīng xióng | a heroine |
| 餐巾 | cān jīn | napkin |
| 手巾 | shǒu jīn | hand towel |
| 头巾 | tóu jīn | headdress |
| 围巾 | wéi jīn | scarf |

*Example:*

她 用 手 巾 抹 脸 。

Tā yòng shǒu jīn ma liǎn

She uses the towel to wipe her face.

32

## 布 BÙ

cloth

THIS character is based on the radical for cloth: 巾. The phonetic 父 (father) is discernible as 又 in the seal form 术. 又 is a picture of the right hand ( 又 ) with the rod of authority ( | ), and implies discipline, control and order — as essential in weaving as in marrying. So the saying goes: "Hasty weaving produces shoddy cloth; a girl who marries in haste has a fool for a husband."

一 ナ ナ 右 布

| 布道 | bù dào | preach |
| 布丁 | bù dīng | pudding |
| 布防 | bù fáng | place troops on garrison duty |
| 布告 | bù gào | notice; bulletin; proclamation |
| 布谷鸟 | bù gǔ niǎo | cuckoo |
| 布匹 | bù pǐ | cloth; piece goods |
| 布置 | bù zhì | fix up; arrange; decorate; assign; make arrangements for; give instructions about |

*Example:*

用 这 匹 布 做 成 衣 服 ， 一 定 很 漂 亮 。
Yòng zhè pǐ bù zuò chéng yī fu　yí dìng hěn piào liàng
This cloth will make a pretty dress.

33

**ZHǑU**

帚

broom;
duster

IN the seal form 帚, broom is suggested by a hand ( 又 ) with an improvised broom ( 帚 ) — double cloth ( 巾 ) attached to a handle ( ｜ ). Although a helping hand ( 才 ) can easily turn 帚 (broom) into 掃 (sweep), "no one will sweep a public hall used by everyone."

| 刁 | 刁 | 刁 | 刁 | 刍 | 帚 | 帚 | 帚 | | | | | |
|---|---|---|---|---|---|---|---|---|---|---|---|---|

扫帚　　　sào zhǒu　　　broom
扫帚星　　sào zhǒu xīng　　comet

*Example:*

妈 妈 最 近 买 了 一 把 新 扫 帚 。
Mā ma zuì jìn mǎi le yì bǎ xīn sào zhǒu
Mother bought a new broom recently.

34

# 妇 （婦）

**FÙ** wife; married woman

WOMAN (女) with broom (帚) is the symbol for wife or married woman: 婦, simplified to 妇 — woman (女) with helping hand (⺕). Another character for wife is 妻 — woman (女) with broom (十) in hand (⺕). Whatever the character, "She who is the wife of one man cannot eat the rice of two."

PENG

| 〈 | 乆 | 女 | 妇 | 妇 | 妇 | | | | | | | | | | |
|---|---|---|---|---|---|---|---|---|---|---|---|---|---|---|---|

| 少妇 | shào fù | young married woman |
|---|---|---|
| 夫妇 | fū fù | husband and wife |
| 妇产科 | fù chǎn kē | (department of) gynaecology and obstetrics |
| 妇女 | fù nǚ | woman |
| 妇人 | fù rén | married woman |
| 妇幼 | fù yòu | women and children |

*Example:*

这 位 少 妇 真 勇 敢 ， 为 了 丈 夫 不 惜 牺 牲 一 切 。

Zhè wèi shào fù zhēn yǒng gǎn wéi le zhàng fū bù xì xī shēng yí qiè

She's a brave young woman. She sacrificed herself for the sake of her husband.

## 帝 DÌ emperor

CREATING a symbol to suit the emperor can be a thorny problem. The ancient forms 帝 and 帝 represented him with long robes and designated by 一 (上, superior). Two arms were later added: 帝. Then the bottom was changed to 朿 (朿, thorns) to produce 帝 and finally 帝. Hence the saying: "To attend on the emperor is like sleeping with a tiger."

| 皇帝 | huáng dì | emperor |
| 上帝 | shàng dì | God |
| 帝国 | dì guó | empire |
| 帝国主义 | dì guó zhǔ yì | imperialism |
| 帝王 | dì wáng | emperor; monarch |
| 帝制 | dì zhì | autocratic monarchy; monarchy |

*Example:*

秦 始 皇 是 中 国 第 一 个 皇 帝 。
Qín shǐ huáng shì Zhōng Guó dì yi ge huáng dì
Qinshihuang was the first emperor of China.

36

**DÀI**  girdle; bring

帯 is a pictograph of the ancient girdle, embellished with trinkets hanging from it: 卅. At the bottom of the character are the robes, represented by 帀 — two 巾, one over the other. 帯 also means to bring or take along, as articles are often carried, tucked in or worn at the girdle.

一 十 卄 卅 卅 芇 芇 芇 带

| 录音带 | lù yīn dài | recording tape |
| 热带 | rè dài | the tropics |
| 带累 | dài lěi | implicate; involve |
| 带领 | dài lǐng | lead; guide |
| 带路 | dài lù | show the way; act as a guide |
| 带头 | dài tóu | take the lead; be the first |

*Example:*

老 师 带 领 一 群 学 生 去 爬 山 。
Lǎo shī dài lǐng yī qún xué shēng qù pá shān
The teacher led a group of students for a climb in the mountain.

**帽** **MÀO**

hat; cap

THE phonetic 冒 means rash, acting with eyes ( 目 ) covered ( 冃 ). 冃 indicates a cover ( 冂 ) for something ( 一 ), viz., the head ( 一 ). 冒 combines with the radical 巾 (cloth) to produce 帽 (hat, cap). A cap does not always fit the head of the wearer because "many a good man can be found under a shabby hat."

| 丨 | 冂 | 巾 | 巾丶 | 巾冂 | 巾冃 | 帽 | 巾冃 | 帽 | 帽 | 帽 | 帽 | | |

| | | |
|---|---|---|
| 安全帽 | ān chuán mào | safety helmet |
| 帽徽 | mào huī | insignia on a cap |
| 帽子 | mào zi | headgear; hat; cap; label; tag; brand |

*Example:*

当 上 工 地 时 ， 请 记 得 带 上 安 全 帽 。
Dāng shàng gōng dì shí   qǐng jì dé dài shàng ān quán mào
Please remember to put on the safety helmet when you are at the work site.

38

**CHÁNG**       always; constantly

常 is made up of the radical 巾 (cloth) and phonetic 尚 (elevated). 尚 is a picture of the upper part of a house with a roof (宀), a smoke hole (口) and a ridge (丨) which divides (八) wind and rain. 巾 represents the banner raised as a signal in front of the general's headquarters 尚 and which flies constantly: 常.

| | | | | | | | | | | | | |
|---|---|---|---|---|---|---|---|---|---|---|---|---|
| 丨 | 冖 | 丷 | 丷 | 业 | 尚 | 尚 | 尚 | 常 | 常 | 常 | | |

| | | | |
|---|---|---|---|
| 常备军 | cháng bèi jūn | standing army |
| 常常 | cháng cháng | frequently; generally |
| 常会 | cháng huì | regular meeting |
| 常见 | cháng jiàn | common |
| 常年 | cháng nián | throughout the year; perennial |
| 常人 | cháng rén | man in the street |
| 常识 | cháng shí | general or elementary knowledge |
| 常态 | cháng tài | normal behaviour or conditions |
| 常务 | cháng wù | day-to-day business; routine |
| 常言道 | cháng yán dào | as the saying goes |
| 常用 | cháng yòng | in common use |
| 常驻 | cháng zhù | resident; permanent |

*Example:*

她 常 常 去 听 音 乐 会 。

Tā cháng cháng qu tīng yīn yuè huà

She goes to the concerts very often.

39

# 帮 (幫)

**BĀNG**　　　help; assist

IN feudal times the emperor relied on the support of his nobles. The seal form of the character for such aid combines 坴 with 帛 . 坴 denotes the crops (坴) and land (土) under the noble's rule (彐). 帛 signifies the silk or wealth donated.

In the modern form the phonetic 邦 means state or country represented by woods (丰) and city (阝).

| 一 | 二 | 三 | 丰 | 邦 | 邦 | 邦 | 帮 | 帮 | | | | |
|---|---|---|---|---|---|---|---|---|---|---|---|---|

| 帮忙 | bāng máng | help; give a hand; do a favour |
|---|---|---|
| 帮手 | bāng shou | helper; assistant |
| 帮凶 | bāng xiōng | accomplice; accessary |
| 帮助 | bāng zhù | help; assist |

*Example:*

我 想 把 这 箱 水 果 搬 到 那 里 ， 你 能 帮 我 吗 ？

Wǒ xiǎng bǎ zhè xiāng shuǐ guǒ bān dào nà lǐ　　nǐ néng bāng wǒ ma

Can you help me to carry the carton of fruits there?

40

衣 **YĪ** clothes

衣 delineates the outlines of clothing: on the top, the outer garments with sleeves; at the bottom, the flowing robes. This pictograph serves as a radical for characters relating to clothing. Apparently, clothes do not make the man, according to the saying: "You can change the clothes; you cannot change the man."

`ˋ` `一` `ナ` `才` `衤` `衣`

| 衣橱 | yī chú | wardrobe |
| 衣服 | yī fu | clothing; clothes |
| 衣冠楚楚 | yī guān chǔ chǔ | be immaculately dressed |
| 衣冠禽兽 | yī guān qín shòu | a beast in human attire; brute |
| 衣架 | yī jià | coat hanger; clothes-rack |
| 衣食住行 | yī shí zhù xíng | food, clothing, shelter and transportation — basic necessities of life |
| 衣鱼 | yī yú | silverfish; fish moth; bookworm |

*Example:*

这 件 衣 服 是 新 买 的 ！
Zhè jiàn yī fu shì xīn mǎi de
This dress is newly bought!

41

# 裤 （褲）

**KÙ**     trousers

褲, meaning trousers, is based on the radical 衣 (clothing). The ample storage space of loose Chinese trousers is suggested by the phonetic 庫 (store). 褲 may also be written: 裤, the phonetic 夸 meaning big (大) talk or exclamation (亏).

衫 or robe, the other basic article of clothing (衣), is likened to feathers (彡) that warm the body.

`、　ナ　才　齐　齐　衤　衤　初　栌　桩　裤　裤`

| 短裤 | duǎn kù | shorts |
| 裤子 | kù zi | trousers; pants |

*Example:*

这 条 裤 子 太 短 了 ， 不 能 穿 。
Zhè tiáo kù zi tài duǎn le    bù néng chuāng
This pair of pants is too short.

被 **BÈI**

bedclothes; blankets

被, bedclothes or blankets, are regarded as cloth (衣) skin (皮). The phonetic 皮 or 殳, represents the skin (彡) flayed by hand (又) with knife (⊃). 被 may also mean to suffer, a sign of the passive. However, 袍 (literally, cloth 衣 wrap 包) refers to the long robe or outer garment wrapped round the body to keep it warm and active.

丶 冫 礻 礻 礻 礻 衤 初 初 袯 被

| | | | |
|---|---|---|---|
| 被捕 | bèi bǔ | be arrested; be under arrest |
| 被单 | bèi dān | (bed) sheet |
| 被动 | bèi dòng | passive |
| 被俘 | bèi fú | be captured; be taken prisoner |
| 被告 | bèi gào | defendant; the accused |
| 被害人 | bèi hài rén | the injured party; the victim |
| 被迫 | bèi pò | be compelled; be forced; be constrained |
| 被褥 | bèi rù | bedding; bedclothes |

*Example:*

天 气 好 冷 ， 记 得 盖 被 。
Tiān qì hǎo lěng   jì de gài bèi
It's cold. Remember to pull up your blanket.

## BIǎO

表

express;
show;
manifest

表 combining 衣 with 毛, means to show or make known. Clothes (衣) were originally skins with hair (毛) on the outside. 表 literally means the outside of clothes — the manifestation or outer appearance which may be a false front. It is said that when a boy is small you can see the man, but "A man cannot be known by his looks, nor can the sea be measured with a bushel basket."

一 二 十 主 耂 耒 表 表

| | | | |
|---|---|---|---|
| 表层 | biǎo céng | surface layer | |
| 表达 | biǎo dá | express; convey; voice | |
| 表格 | biǎo gé | form; table | |
| 表决 | biǎo jué | decide by vote; vote | |
| 表露 | biǎo lù | show; reveal | |
| 表面 | biǎo miàn | surface; face; outside; appearance | |

| | | |
|---|---|---|
| 表明 | biǎo míng | make known; make clear |
| 表亲 | biǎo qīn | cousin; cousinship |
| 表情 | biǎo qíng | express one's feelings; expression |
| 表示 | biǎo shì | show; express; indicate |
| 表现 | biǎo xiàn | manifestation; display; manifest |

*Example:*

对 这 问 题 他 没 有 表 明 立 场 。
Duì zhè wèn tí tā méi yǒu biǎo míng lì chǎng
He did not express his stand on this matter.

片

Man cannot wait to saw a tree (木) vertically into two halves: 爿 and 片. 爿 serves as a strong plank for his bed and 片 as a symbol for a slice or piece. With 爿 and 片 he forms a tripod for an urn: 鼎. He uses 木 and its components 爿 and 片 as radicals. And so the saying goes: "He plants a tree in the morning and wants to saw planks from it in the evening."

**PIÀN**   slice; piece

丿 丿' 丿＇ 广 片

| 片段 | piàn duàn | part; passage; extract; fragment |
| 片刻 | piàn kè | a short while; an instant; a moment |
| 片时 | piàn shí | a short while; a moment |
| 片瓦无存 | piàn wǎ wú cún | not a single tile remains — be razed to the ground |
| 片言 | piàn yán | a few words; a phrase or two |
| 片子 | piàn zi | flat, thin piece; slice; flake; scrap |

*Example:*

他 在 这 里 逗 留 了 片 刻 。
Tā zài zhè lǐ dòu liú le piàn kè
He was here for a short while.

45

**床 (牀)**

**CHUÁNG** bed

爿, the left half of a tree (木), represents a thick, strong plank used for a bed. By adding 爿 to 木 you can make 牀 (bed) — literally, strong plank (爿) of wood (木). Another way is by placing 木 (wood) under 广 (roof): 床. As you make your bed, you must lie on it, so "if you can't sleep, don't complain about your bed."

| 、 | 一 | 广 | 广 | 庁 | 庁 | 床 | | | | | | |
|---|---|---|---|---|---|---|---|---|---|---|---|---|

| 单人床 | dān rén chuáng | single bed |
|---|---|---|
| 双人床 | shuāng rén chuáng | double bed |
| 床单 | chuáng dān | bedsheet |
| 床垫 | chuáng diàn | mattress |
| 床位 | chuáng wèi | berth; bunk; bed |
| 床罩 | chuáng zhào | bedspread |

*Example:*

他 卧 病 在 床 。
Tā wò bìng zài chuáng
He is sick in bed.

46

# 墙（牆）

**QIÁNG** wall

THE seal form of the phonetic 嗇 signifies grain (来) stored within (入) a double-walled granary (回). The idea of wall is reinforced by the radical 爿, a symbol of strength. Since walls are made of clay or earth (土), the character may also be written: 墙. Walls may fortify a city, but "men, not walls, make a city."

一 十 土 圹 圹 圹 坮 埒 埒 墙 墙 墙 墙

| 墙壁 | qiáng bì | wall |
| 墙角 | qiáng jiǎo | a corner formed by two walls |
| 墙脚 | qiáng jiǎo | the foot of a wall; foundation |

*Example·*

墙 壁 上 有 一 个 大 洞 。
Qiáng bì shang yǒu yī ge dà dòng
There is a big hole on the wall.

将 (將)

将 has many seal forms and varied meanings:
is a meatblock ( 月 ) with meat ( 肉 ).
shows the meatblock ( 月 ) with meat ( 夕 ) and salt ( 卤 ).
represents the meatblock ( 月 ) with meat ( 夕 ) and brine ( 酉 ).
signifies the hand ( 寸 ) placing meat ( 夕 ) upon the block ( 月 ).

**JIĀNG**   take; hold; handle; shall; will

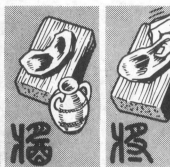

Hence the extended meanings: offer, present; nourish, help; take, hold; handle, manage. 将 is a character with a future, often used for shall or will; it is even used to mean leader or general.

PENG

丶　丶　丬　丬　丬ゝ　丬夕　丬夕　将　将

| 将错就错 | jiāng cuò jiù cuò | leave a mistake uncorrected and make the best of it |
| 将计就计 | jiāng jì jiù jì | turn somebody's trick against him; beat somebody at his own game |
| 将近 | jiāng jìn | close to; nearly; almost |
| 将军 | jiāng jūn | general |
| 将来 | jiāng lái | future |

*Example:*

我　将　请　他　来　我　家　。
Wǒ  jiāng  qǐng  tā  lái  wǒ  jiā
I am inviting him over to my house.

# 壮 (壯)

**ZHUÀNG**

strong;
eminent;
impressive

壯 literally means a strong and impressive ( 爿 ) personage ( 士 ) or one who professes to be so; by extension, strong and able-bodied.

An analogous character is 妝 (adorn, disguise) — an impressive ( 爿 ) woman ( 女 ), i.e., one who adorns herself with make-up.

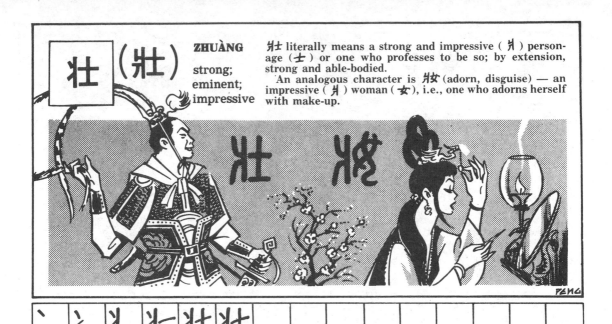

| 壮胆 | zhuàng dǎn | embolden; boost somebody's courage |
| 壮丽 | zhuàng lì | majestic; magnificent; glorious |
| 壮烈 | zhuàng liè | heroic; brave |
| 壮士 | zhuàng shì | hero; warrior |
| 壮实 | zhuàng shi | sturdy; robust |
| 壮志 | zhuàng zhì | great aspiration; lofty ideal |

*Example:*

他 为 国 壮 烈 牺 牲 。
Tā wèi guó zhuàng liè xī shēng
He sacrificed heroically for his country.

# 装 (裝)

**ZHUĀNG** pack; fill; pretend

壯, the phonetic, means strong or robust. It was originally applied to an official distinguished by his robe of office, and therefore has to do with appearance. The addition of the radical 衣 (clothing) suggests putting oneself into another's clothing and filling it — to deceive; by extension, to pack, fill, pretend: 裝.

`丶` `冫` `ㄤ` `ㄤ-` `卅` `壯` `壯` `壯-` `裝` `裝` `裝`

| | | | |
|---|---|---|---|
| 装扮 | zhuāng bàn | dress up; disguise | |
| 装备 | zhuāng bèi | equip; equipment; outfit | |
| 装糊涂 | zhuāng hú tu | pretend not to know | |
| 装货 | zhuāng huò | loading (cargo) | |
| 装甲车 | zhuāng jiǎ chē | armoured car | |
| 装模作样 | zhuāng mú zuò yàng | be affected; put on an act | |
| 装配 | zhuāng pèi | assemble; fit together | |

| | | |
|---|---|---|
| 装腔 | zhuāng qiāng | behave affectedly; be artificial |
| 装饰 | zhuāng shì | decorate; adorn; ornament; deck |
| 装束 | zhuāng shù | dress; attire |
| 装修 | zhuāng xiū | fit up (a house, etc.) |
| 装置 | zhuāng zhì | install; fit; installation |

*Example:*

她 装 老 大 娘 真 象 。

Tā zhuāng Lǎo dà niáng zhēn xiàng

She acted like an old lady.

**夕**

**XĪ**

evening

夕 is a picture of the crescent moon emerging on the horizon at dusk, its lower part obstructed by a mountain. Hence the extended meaning: dusk, evening. To man, the rising moon presents opportunities but the proverb laments: "How seldom in life is the moon directly overhead!"

| ノ | 勹 | 夕 | | | | | | | | | |
|---|---|---|---|---|---|---|---|---|---|---|---|

| 一朝一夕 | yī zhāo yī xī | overnight |
|---|---|---|
| 夕烟 | xī yān | evening mist |
| 夕阳 | xī yáng | the setting sun |
| 夕照 | xī zhào | the glow of the setting sun; evening glow |

*Example:*

这 些 问 题 不 是 一 朝 一 夕 能 够 解 决 的 。
Zhè xiē wèn tí bú shì yī zhāo yī xī néng gòu jiě jué de
These problems cannot be solved overnight.

**DUŌ**

**many; much**

From morning to evening man toiled in the field, and evening ( 夕 ) after evening ( 夕 ) he noted the fruitage of his labour. "Many evenings" ( 多 ) soon came to mean "many". His hard work bore much ( 多 ) fruit ( 果 ), producing a new word: 夥 (fruitful) and demonstrating the principle: "Sow much, reap much; sow little, reap little."

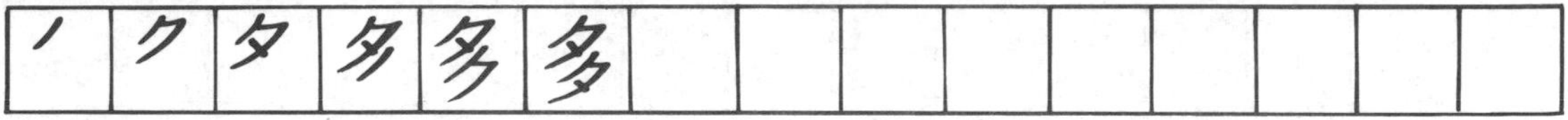

ノ  ク  夕  �  多  多

| | | | |
|---|---|---|---|
| 多半 | duō bàn | the greater part; most | |
| 多才多艺 | duō cái duō yì | versatile; gifted in many ways | |
| 多此一举 | duō cǐ yī jǔ | make an unnecessary move | |
| 多方面 | duō fāng miàn | many-sided; in many ways | |
| 多国公司 | duō guó gōng sī | multinational corporation | |
| 多民族 | duō mín zú | | |
| 国家 | guó jiā | multinational country | |

| | | |
|---|---|---|
| 多少 | duō shǎo | amount; somewhat; how many |
| 多时 | duō shí | a long time |
| 多谢 | duō xiè | thanks a lot |
| 多心 | duō xīn | oversensitive; suspicious |
| 多余 | duō yú | unnecessary; superfluous |
| 多嘴 | duō zuǐ | speak out of turn |

*Example:*

你 的 担 心 是 多 余 的 。

Ni  de  dān  xīn  shì  dūo  yú  de

Your worries are unnecessary.

52

**夠**

**GÒU**
enough

句 is to hook ( 勹 ) with the mouth ( 口 ): to entice; 多 means much, many. 夠 therefore signifies to entice many, i.e., enough. But enough is not always enough, according to the proverb: "To complete a thing, a hundred years is not sufficient; to destroy it, a day is more than enough."

ノ 勹 夕 夕 多 多 多 夗 夠 夠 夠

| 够本 | gòu běn | break even |
| 够朋友 | gòu péng you | be a friend indeed |
| 够受的 | gòu shòu de | quite an ordeal |
| 够意思 | gòu yì si | really something; terrific; generous; really kind |

*Example:*

这 场 球 赛 可 真 够 意 思 。
Zhè cháng qiú sài kě zhēn gòu yì sì
That was really a terrific game.

53

**DIĒ**

**father;**
**daddy**

It takes three desperate characters to represent father:
父 is raised hand (又) wielding a rod ( l ).
爹 incorporates 多 — much raising of hand with rod.
爸 includes 巴 — poised like a snake, ready to strike.
All of them exemplify the saying, "It is easier to rule a nation than a son."

| 爸爸 | bà ba | papa; dad; father |
| 爹爹 | diē die | father; dad; papa |
| 爹娘 | diē niáng | parents |
| 父老 | fù lǎo | elders (of a country or district) |
| 父母 | fù mǔ | father and mother; parents |
| 父亲 | fù qīn | father |
| 父系亲属 | fù xì qīn shǔ | relatives on the paternal side |

*Example:*

父 亲 节 那 天 ， 我 送 爸 爸 一 份 礼 物 。
Fù qīn jié nà tiān wǒ sòng bà ba yí fèn lǐ wù
On Father's Day, I gave my father a present.

54

**WÀI**
outside

外 is composed of 夕 (evening) and 卜 (divine). Divination ( 卜 ), by interpreting the vertical ( 丨 ) and horizontal ( - ) cracks of a heated tortoise-shell, was deemed effective only before (or outside of) evening. Hence the meaning: outside or foreign. And for such outside or foreign help, many will pay handsomely — those who place trust in the saying: "Much money moves the gods."

| ノ | ク | 夕 | 列 | 外 | | | | | | | | | |

| 外币 | wài bì | foreign currency | 外交 | wài jiāo | diplomacy; foreign affairs |
|------|--------|-------------------|------|----------|------------------------------|
| 外边 | wài bian | outside; out | 外快 | wài kuài | extra income |
| 外表 | wài biǎo | outward appearance; exterior | 外贸 | wài mào | foreign trade |
| 外宾 | wài bīn | foreign guest | 外貌 | wài mào | appearance; looks |
| 外公 | wài gōng | (maternal) grandfather | 外人 | wài rén | stranger; outsider |
| 外国 | wài guó | foreign country | 外孙 | wài sūn | daughter's son; grandson |
| 外行 | wài háng | layman; nonprofessional | 外套 | wài tào | overcoat |
| 外籍 | wài jí | foreign nationality | | | |

*Example:*

我 对 音 乐 很 外 行 。
Wǒ duì yīn yùe hěn wài háng
I am a layman in music.

55

# 梦（夢）

**MÈNG**    dream

The seal forms of dream are horrifying enough to evoke a nightmare. No wonder the original character; 瞢 means bad sight ( 苜 ) with covered ( 冖 ) eyes ( 目 ). Dreams being evening visions, 夕 replaces 目 in the new form: 夢, now simplified to 梦 (evening trees) — a pleasant dream. Unfortunately, "a beautiful dream is soon ended."

| 梦话 | mèng huà | words uttered in one's sleep; somniloquy |
| 梦幻 | mèng huàn | illusion; dream; reverie |
| 梦境 | mèng jìng | dreamland; dreamworld; dream |
| 梦想 | mèng xiǎng | dream of; vainly hope |
| 梦游症 | mèng yóu zhèng | somnambulism; sleepwalking |

*Example:*

昨 晚 我 听 见 你 说 梦 话 。

Zuó wǎn wǒ tīng jiàn nǐ shuō mèng huà

I heard you talk in your sleep last night.

56

# 夜

**YÈ**

night

The seal character 夜 depicts man ( 大 ) sleeping on his side ( ノ ) in the evening ( 夕 ). The modern form 夜 shows man ( 亻 ) under cover ( 亠 ) lying on his other side ( 乀 ) also in the evening ( 夕 ). If night can be suggested by sleep, as in both these forms, then day can be transformed into night, as demonstrated by our sleepy characters shown here.

丶 亠 广 亠 衤 夜 夜 夜

| 开夜车 | kāi yè chē | work deep into the night; burn the midnight oil |
| 夜班 | yè bān | night shift |
| 夜半 | yè bàn | midnight |
| 夜长梦多 | yè cháng mèng duō | a long night is fraught with dreams – a long delay means many hitches |
| 夜工 | yè gōng | night job |
| 夜盲 | yè máng | night blindness |
| 夜勤 | yè qín | night duty |
| 夜晚 | yè wǎn | night |
| 夜以继日 | yè yǐ jì rì | day and night; round the clock |

*Example:*

工 程 正 在 夜 以 继 日 地 进 行 。

Gōng chéng zhèng zài yè yǐ jì rì de jìn xíng

Work is going on day and night at the construction site.

57

## 名

**MÍNG**     name; fame

In the dusk (夕), man is not clearly discernible, so he identifies himself, announcing by word of mouth (口) his name: 名. And if he has a good name and reputation, he has nothing to fear. Let him draw courage from the saying: "Travelling or at home, the gentleman does not change his name."

ノ　ク　夕　夕　名　名

| | | | |
|---|---|---|---|
| 名不虚传 | míng bù xū chuán | live up to one's reputation | |
| 名册 | míng cè | register | |
| 名产 | míng chǎn | famous product | |
| 名称 | míng chēng | name (of a thing or organization) | |
| 名单 | míng dān | name list | |
| 名贵 | míng guì | famous and precious; rare | |

| | | |
|---|---|---|
| 名教 | míng jiào | the Confucian ethical code |
| 名流 | míng liú | distinguished personages |
| 名牌 | míng pái | famous brand |
| 名片 | míng piàn | visiting card; calling card |
| 名声 | míng shēng | reputation; repute; renown |
| 名胜 | míng shèng | a place famous for its scenery or historical relics |

*Example:*

他 用 的 是 一 辆 名 牌 的 车 子 。
Tā yòng de shì yí liàng míng pái de chē zi
The car he is using is of a famous brand.

 **MÍNG**

inscribe; engrave

Name (名) on metal or gold (金) means to carve, inscribe or engrave: 铭. Because a good name is worth more than gold, it is durable, unlike the rotten one referred to in the proverb: "Decayed wood cannot be carved."

丿 𠂉 𠂆 𠂢 𠂤 钅 钆 钇 钉 铭 铭

| 铭诸肺腑 | míng zhū fèi fǔ | engrave on one's mind (memory); bear firmly in mind |
| 铭感 | míng gǎn | be deeply grateful |
| 铭记 | míng jì | engrave on one's mind; always remember |
| 铭刻 | míng kè | inscription; always remember |
| 铭文 | míng wén | inscription; epigraph |

*Example:*

他 把 母 亲 的 教 诲 铭 诸 肺 腑 。
Tā bǎ mǔ qin de jiào huì míng zhū fèi fǔ
He bore his mother's teachings firmly in mind.

**YUÀN**

hatred;
resentment

This character is based on 心 (heart), the seat of feelings. The phonetic indicates a turning away (巳) from someone hateful, acting as if it were night (夕) and calling it a day. If such hatred or resentment leads to violence, remember the counsel: "An angry fist cannot strike a smiling face."

ノ　ク　タ　タ］　夗　怨　怨　怨　怨

| 怨不得 | yuàn bu de | cannot blame |
| 怨愤 | yuàn fèn | discontent and indignation |
| 怨恨 | yuàn hèn | have a grudge against somebody; hate; resentment |
| 怨气 | yuàn qì | grievance; complaint; resentment |
| 怨天尤人 | yuàn tiān yóu rén | blame god and man — blame everyone and everything but oneself |
| 怨言 | yuàn yán | complaint; grumble |

*Example:*

巴　士　坏　了　，　怨　不　得　他　们　迟　到　。
Bā shì huài le yuàn bu de tā men chí dào
The bus broke down. No wonder they were late.

60

# 从 (從)

**CÓNG**  follow; from

從 represents two men (从) walking ( 彳 ) and stopping ( 止 ). In the seal form, 彳 and 止 are united into 辵 (going). The simplified form is 从 — a man following another man — a simple task, in view of the saying: "To know the truth is easy; but, ah, how difficult it is to follow it!"

PENG

| 丿 | 人 | 从 | 从 | | | | | | | | | | | |
|---|---|---|---|---|---|---|---|---|---|---|---|---|---|---|

| | | | | | |
|---|---|---|---|---|---|
| 从容 | cōng róng | calm; unhurried; leisurely | 从事 | cóng shì | go in for; be engaged in |
| 从此 | cóng cǐ | from this time on; henceforth | 从属 | cóng shǔ | subordinate |
| 从简 | cóng jiǎn | conform to the principle of simplicity | 从速 | cóng sù | as soon as possible |
| 从军 | cóng jūn | join the army; enlist | 从头 | cóng tóu | from the beginning; anew |
| 从来 | cóng lái | always; at all times; all along | 从小 | cóng xiǎo | from childhood; as a child |
| 从前 | cóng qián | before; formerly; in the past | 从中 | cóng zhōng | out of; from among |

*Example:*

我 从 来 没 有 见 过 他 。
Wǒ cóng lái méi yǒu jiàn gūo tā
I have never seen him before.

# 行

**XÍNG** walk; go

**HÁNG** shop; trade

Originally this was a pictograph of a cross-road: 𢌿. Now it is a radical which combines one step with the left foot (彳) and one step with the right (亍) to suggest walk, go or travel: 行. Since business thrives at cross-roads, 行 can apply to shop, trade or business, on the basis of the saying: "If a little money does not go out, great money will not come in."

丶　丿　彳　彳　行　行

| 行家 | háng jia | expert |
| 行列 | háng liè | ranks |
| 行情 | háng qíng | quotations (on the market); prices |
| 行业 | háng yè | trade; profession; industry |
| 行长 | háng zhǎng | president (of a bank) |
| 行不通 | xíng bu tōng | won't do or work; get nowhere |
| 行人 | xíng rén | pedestrian |
| 行政 | xíng zhèng | administration |

*Example:*

请 问 你 是 从 事 什 么 行 业 的 ?

Qǐng wèn nǐ shì cóng shì shén me háng yè de

May I know your profession?

62

**得**

**DÉ** get; obtain

彳, the radical, means step. The phonetic 㝵 — to lay hands (寸) on what one has in view (見 or 旦) — signifies to obtain. However, laying hands on money is not easy: "Money comes like earth picked up with a pin, but goes like sand washed away by water."

ノ 丿 彳 彳 彳 彳 彳 得 得 得 得

| | | | |
|---|---|---|---|
| 得寸进尺 | dé cùn jìn chǐ | give him an inch and he"ll take an ell; be insatiable | |
| 得到 | dé dào | get; obtain; gain; receive | |
| 得分 | dé fēn | score | |
| 得奖 | dé jiǎng | win or be awarded a prize | |
| 得胜 | dé shèng | win a victory; triumph | |
| 得失 | dé shī | gain and loss; success and failure | |

| | | |
|---|---|---|
| 得势 | dé shì | be in power; get the upper hand |
| 得悉 | dé xī | hear of; learn about |
| 得益 | dē yì | benefit; profit |
| 得志 | dé zhì | achieve one's ambition |
| 得罪 | dé zuì | offend; displease |

*Example:*

两 种 办 法 各 有 得 失 。

Liáng zhǒng bàn fǎ gè yǒu dé shī

Each of the two methods has its advantages and disadvantages.

**DÉ**

virtue; goodness

直 means straight ( 一 ) as tested by ten ( 十 ) eyes ( 目 ). 心 is the heart. So the phonetic 惪 denotes a straight heart. Clarified by the radical for step ( 彳 ) to mean the way to virtue or goodness, 德 is defined by the saying: "To talk good is not being good; to do good, that is being good."

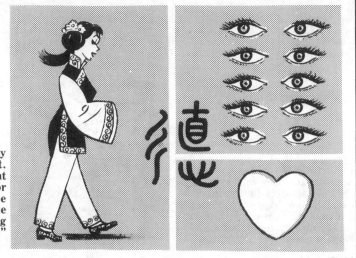

PENG

丿 丿 彳 彳 彳 彳 徝 徝 徝 徝 徝 德 德 德

| 德高望重 | dé gāo wàng zhòng | be of noble character and high prestige |
| 德国 | Dé Guó | Germany |
| 德行 | dé xíng | moral integrity; moral conduct |
| 德育 | dé yù | moral education |
| 品德 | pǐn dé | moral character |

*Example:*

政 府 现 在 正 在 积 极 推 行 德 育 。
Zhèng fǔ xiàn zài zhèng zài jī jí tuī xíng dé yù
The government is at present actively promoting moral education.

**TÚ**

徒

follower;
go on foot

The seal form of 走 is 夳 — a man bending forward (夭) to go on foot, (止) i.e., walk. The seal form of 徒, however, is 尯 — one who goes (夆) on the ground, (土) i.e., a disciple who walks in the footsteps of his master, like the shadow following the substance.

ノ ク イ 彳 彳 往 往 徒 徒

| 徒步 | tú bù | on foot |
| 徒弟 | tú di | apprentice; disciple |
| 徒工 | tú gōng | apprentice |
| 徒劳 | tú láo | futile effort; fruitless labour |

*Example:*

他 已 尽 了 力 ， 到 最 后 还 是 徒 劳 无 功 。
Tā yǐ jìn le lì  dào zuì hòu hái shì tú láo wú gōng
He has tried his best but to no avail.

65

# 很

**HĚN**

very; quite

The phonetic 艮 (originally 㫗) means stubborn — to turn around (匕) and eye (目) another defiantly. The radical 彳 (step) suggests the steps needed to curb this stubbornness; hence intensive, very. An analogous character is 狠 — obstinate (艮) and beastly (犭).

PENG

丿 亻 彳 彳 彳 彳 很 很 很

| 好得很 | hǎo de hěn | very good |
| 很有道理 | hěn yǒu dào li | contain much truth; be quite correct |

*Example:*

他 的 上 司 对 他 的 工 作 表 现 感 到 很 满 意 。

Tā de shàng si duì tā de gōng zuò biǎo xiàn gǎn dào hěn mǎn yì

His boss is very pleased with his work performance.

## 街 JIĒ
road; street

行, the radical, represents footprints; it means to go, walk or travel. The phonetic 圭 (soil 土 doubled) suggests road, street or ground for walking. Travelling on a road can be trying, hence: "Long roads test the horse; long dealings test the friend."

ノ ノ 彳 彳 彳 往 往 往 徉 徍 街 街

| 街道 | jiē dào | street; residential district; neighbourhood |
| 街坊 | jiē fang | neighbour |
| 街市 | jiē shì | downtown streets |
| 街头 | jiē tóu | street corner; street |
| 街头巷尾 | jiē tóu xiàng wěi | streets and lanes |

*Example:*

街 头 巷 尾 ， 到 处 都 是 欢 乐 的 人 群 。
Jiē tóu xiàng wěi    dào chù dōu shì huān lè de rén qún

There are happy crowds in all the streets and lanes.

67

# 律

**LÜ**

law; rule
discipline

The phonetic 聿 signifies written regulations — hand ( 彐 ) with pen ( 丨 ) writing lines ( 一 ) on tablet ( 一 ). The radical 彳 (step) suggests steps taken to enforce them as law to protect the citizens. However, "Going to the law is losing a cow for the sake of a cat."

丿 ⺈ 彳 彳 彳 彳 彳 律 律

| 律吕 | lǜ lǚ | bamboo pitch-pipes used in ancient China; temperament |
| 律师 | lǜ shī | lawyer; barrister; solicitor |
| 律诗 | lǜ shī | a poem of eight lines, each containing five or seven characters, with a strict tonal pattern and rhyme scheme |

*Example:*

辩 方 律 师 为 被 告 辩 护 。

Biàn fāng lǜ shī wèi bèi gào biàn hù

The lawyer speaks in defence of the accused.

**HOU**
after; behind

This character combines three signs: 彳 (step with left foot), 幺 (the finest thread, least or last) and 夂 (hindered at the feet from behind). All three factors contribute to the sense: behind, after or future. 後 is now simplified to 后 (empress) probably because the queen goes after the king in traditional China.

| | | | |
|---|---|---|---|
| 后半 | hòu bàn | latter half; second half |
| 后备军 | hòu bèi jūn | reserves; reserve force |
| 后辈 | hòu bèi | younger generation; posterity |
| 后代 | hòu dài | later periods (in history) |
| 后方 | hòu fāng | rear |
| 后跟 | hòu gēn | heel (of a shoe or sock) |
| 后果 | hòu guǒ | consequence; aftermath |

| | | |
|---|---|---|
| 后患 | hòu huàn | future trouble |
| 后悔 | hòu huǐ | regret; repent |
| 后会有期 | hòu huì yǒu qī | we'll meet again some day |
| 后景 | hòu jǐng | background |
| 后来 | hòu lái | afterwards; later |
| 后天 | hòu tiān | day after tomorrow; postnatal; acquired |

*Example:*

知 识 是 后 天 获 得 的 ， 不 是 先 天 就 有 的 。
Zhī shi shì hòu tiān huò dé de　　bú shi xiān tiān jiù yǒu de
Knowledge is acquired, not innate.

69

# 待

**DÀI**

treat;  deal with

寺 is a court where the law or rule (寸) is applied continually, like the growth of a plant (虫). The radical 彳 indicates the step or way to treat others with propriety, requiring patience and application of the golden rule: "Do to others as you would have them do to you."

PENG

丿 勹 彳 彳 彳 彳 往 待 待

| 待命 | dài mìng | await orders |
| 待人接物 | dài rén jiē wù | the way one gets along with people |
| 待续 | dài xù | to be continued |
| 待遇 | dài yù | treatment; remuneration |

*Example:*

这 间 公 司 对 职 员 很 照 顾 ， 给 的 待 遇 也 很 好 。
Zhè jiān gōng sī duì zhí yuán hěn zhào gu    gěi de dài yù yě hěn hǎo
This company treats its employees well, and also offers attractive remuneration.

70

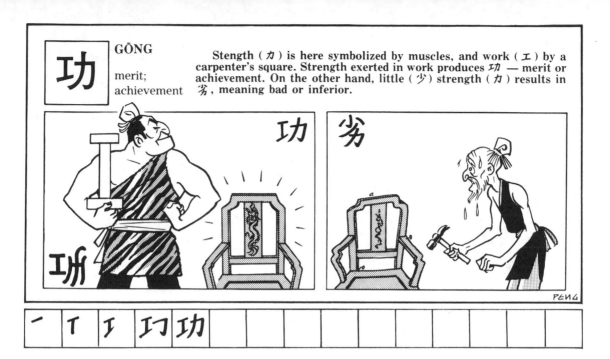

**功** GŌNG

merit;
achievement

Stength ( 力 ) is here symbolized by muscles, and work ( 工 ) by a carpenter's square. Strength exerted in work produces 功 — merit or achievement. On the other hand, little ( 少 ) strength ( 力 ) results in 劣, meaning bad or inferior.

一　丁　工　功　功

| 功败垂成 | gōng bài chuí chéng | fail in a great undertaking on the verge of success |
| 功德 | gōng dé | merits and virtues |
| 功课 | gōng kè | schoolwork; homework |
| 功亏一篑 | gōng kuī yī kuì | fall short of success for lack of a final effort |
| 功劳 | gōng láo | contribution; meritorious service; credit |
| 功能 | gōng néng | function |
| 功效 | gōng xiào | efficacy; effect |

*Example:*

她 的 功 劳 可 不 小 啊 ！

Tā　de　gōng　lao　kě　bù　xiǎo　ǎ

She has certainly made no small contribution!

## 加 JIĀ

add;
increase

This ideograph means to add to or increase. It adds strength ( 力 ) to mouth ( 口 ) by applying force to words. Adding violence to persuasion cannot always be justified. Although might is never right, right is always might.

PENG

| フ | カ | か | 加 | 加 | | | | | | | | |

| | | | | | | | |
|---|---|---|---|---|---|---|---|
| 加班 | jiā bān | work overtime | | 加冕 | jiā miǎn | coronation |
| 加倍 | jiā bèi | double; redouble | | 加强 | jiā qiáng | strengthen; enhance |
| 加法 | jiā fǎ | addition | | 加入 | jiā rù | add; mix; join; accede to |
| 加害 | jiā hài | injure; do harm to | | 加速 | jiā sù | accelerate; expedite |
| 加紧 | jiā jǐn | step up; speed up; intensify | | 加意 | jiā yì | with special care; with close attention |
| 加宽 | jiā kuān | broaden; widen | | | | |
| 加仑 | jiā lún | gallon | | 加油 | jiā yóu | refuel; make an extra effort |

*Example:*

观 众 为 运 动 员 们 加 油 。
Guān zhòng wèi yùn dòng yuán men jiā yóu
The spectators cheered the players on.

72

# 办 (辦)

**BÀN**    handle; manage

辛 is one who has offended (羊) a superior (亠 or 上). 𘤩辛 means to handle or manage; literally, to interpose force (力) between two offenders (辛辛). Such man-handling often leads to injury. Better to heed the proverb: "Just scales and full measure injure no man."

ㄱ 力 𘤩 办

| | | |
|---|---|---|
| 办案 | bàn àn | handle a case |
| 办到 | bàn dào | get something done; accomplish |
| 办法 | bàn fǎ | way; means; measure |
| 办公 | bàn gōng | handle official business; work (usually in an office) |
| 办理 | bàn lǐ | handle; conduct; transact |
| 办事 | bàn shì | handle affairs; work |
| 办罪 | bàn zuì | punish |

*Example:*

这 些 事 情 你 可 以 斟 酌 办 理 。
Zhè xiē shì qing ni kě yǐ zhēn zhuó bàn lǐ

You may handle these matters as you see fit.

73

# 协 (協)

**XIÉ**
together;
co-operate

Triple-strength (協), signifying the multiple efforts of ten (十) persons in unity, indicates wholehearted cooperation: 協. Without cooperation, shared responsibility leads to neglect. "If two men feed a horse, it will be thin, if two men mend a boat, it will leak."

一 十 忄 协 协 协

| | | | | | | |
|---|---|---|---|---|---|---|

协定　xié dìng　agreement; accord
协会　xié huì　association; society
协力　xié lì　unite efforts; join in a common effort
协商　xié shāng　consult; talk things over
协调　xié tiáo　coordinate; concert; harmonize

协同　xié tóng　work in coordination with; cooperate with
协议　xié yì　agree on; agreement
协助　xié zhù　assist; help; give assistance
协奏曲　xié zòu qǔ　concerto
协作　xié zuò　cooperation; coordination; combined

*Example:*

体 操 运 动 员 的 动 作 协 调 优 美 。
Tǐ cāo yùn dòng yuán de dòng zuò xié tiáo yōu měi
The gymnast's movements are harmonious and graceful.

74

# 劳 (勞)

**LÁO**   work; labour

勞 is to toil ( 力 ) indoors ( 宀 ) by the light of many fires ( 火火 ). Burning the midnight oil or the candle at both ends is a waste of effort. "It is labour lost, trying to catch the moon in the water or polishing brick to make a mirror."

一 十 卄 艹 艻 劳 劳

| | | | |
|---|---|---|---|
| 劳动 | láo dòng | work; labour |
| 劳而无功 | láo ér wú gōng | work hard but to no avail |
| 劳工 | láo gōng | labourer; worker |
| 劳累 | láo lèi | tired; run-down |
| 劳力 | láo lì | labour; labour force |
| 劳碌 | láo lù | work hard; toil |

| | | |
|---|---|---|
| 劳神 | láo shén | be a tax on (one's mind); bother; trouble |
| 劳心 | láo xīn | work with one's mind or brains |
| 劳燕分飞 | láo yàn fēn fēi | part; separate |
| 劳资 | láo zī | labour and capital |

*Example:*

你 现 在 身 体 不 好 ，  不 要 过 于 劳 神 。

Nǐ xiàn zài shēn tǐ bù hǎo   bù yào guò yú láo shén

You're in poor health; so don't overtax yourself.

75

# 烦（煩）

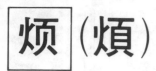

**FÁN**  troubled; irritated

頁 refers to the head (百) upon a body (儿). 火, the radical, represents fire or fever. When you are grieved or irritated, with fire in the head, remember: "Though starving to death, do not steal; though annoyed to death, do not file a lawsuit."

丶 丷 ⺌ 火 灯 灯 灯 炉 烦 烦

| | | | |
|---|---|---|---|
| 烦闷 | fán mèn | be unhappy; be worried | |
| 烦恼 | fán nǎo | be vexed; be worried | |
| 烦扰 | fán rǎo | feel disturbed | |
| 烦冗 | fán rǒng | (of one's affairs) diverse and complicated; (of speech or writing) lengthy and tedious | |
| 烦燥 | fán zào | be fidgety; be agitated | |

*Example:*

某 些 动 物 烦 燥 不 安 可 能 是 地 震 临 震 前 的 预 兆 。
Mǒu xiē dòng wù fán zào bù ān kě néng shì dì zhèn lín zhèn qián de yù zhào
Agitated activity by certain animals may be a sign of an impending earthquake.

76

**光 GUĀNG** light; glory

The ancient form 茣 means twenty ( 廿 ) fires ( 火 ). The modern form 灻 portrays a man ( 儿 ) bearing a torch ( 火 ). Whatever the form, 光 means brightness and glory which, unfortunately, never lasts. Hence: "A bright dawn does not always make a fine day."

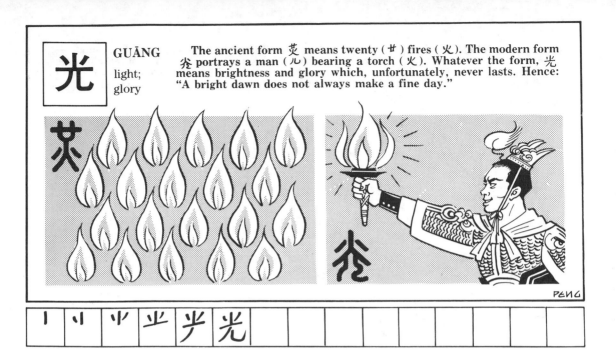

丨 丶丨 丷 丷 丷 光

| | | |
|---|---|---|
| 光彩 | guāng cǎi | lustre; splendour; radiance; honourable; glorious |
| 光辐射 | guāng fù shè | ray radiation |
| 光顾 | guāng gù | patronize |
| 光棍儿 | guāng gùn er | unmarried man; bachelor |
| 光辉 | guāng huī | radiance; brilliance |

| | | |
|---|---|---|
| 光景 | guāng jǐng | scene; circumstances |
| 光芒万丈 | guāng máng wàn zhàng | shining with boundless radiance |
| 光明 | guāng míng | light; bright; promising |
| 光荣 | guāng róng | honour; glory; credit |
| 光天化日 | guāng tiān huà rì | broad daylight |

*Example:*

光 彩 绚 丽 的 贝 雕 吸 引 了 许 多 观 众 。
Guāng cǎi xuàn lì de bèi diāo xī yǐn le xǔ duō guān zhòng
The brilliant lustre of the shell attracted many visitors.

77

# 先

**XIĀN**

first; before

The top part 生 is a small plant ( Ψ ) issuing from the ground ( 一 ); thus indicating progress. The lower part is a picture of marching legs. Accordingly, 先 means to advance ( 生 ) on one's feet ( 儿 ) — to be first. And to progress with people, remember: "Courtesy first, force later" (先 礼 后 兵).

PENG

丿 ⺍ 生 先

| | | | | |
|---|---|---|---|---|
| 先辈 | xiān bèi | elder generation; ancestors |
| 先导 | xiān dǎo | guide; forerunner |
| 先后 | xiān hòu | early or late; priority; one after another |
| 先进 | xiān jìn | advanced |
| 先来后到 | xiān lái hòu dào | first come, first served |
| 先生 | xiān sheng | teacher; mister |
| 先下手为强 | xiān xià shǒu wéi qiáng | he who strikes first gains the advantage |
| 先知 | xiān zhī | person of foresight; prophet |

*Example:*

这 些 事 都 该 办 ； 可 也 得 有 个 先 后 。

Zhè xiē shì dōu gāi bàn　kě yě děi yǒu gè xiān hòu

All these matters should be tackled, but they should be taken up in order of priority.

78

**XǏ** wash; clean

The radical is シ (water) and the phonetic 先 (first). This suggests that you must have water (シ) first (先) to wash or clean: 洗. And what needs to be cleansed first? According to the proverbial exhortation: "Cleanse your heart as you would cleanse a dish."

`丶  丶  氵  氵  氵  汁  汴  洗  洗`

| 洗尘 | xǐ chén | give a dinner of welcome (to a visitor from afar) |
| 洗涤 | xǐ dí | wash; cleanse |
| 洗发剂 | xǐ fà jì | shampoo |
| 洗劫 | xǐ jié | loot; sack |
| 洗刷 | xǐ shuā | wash and brush; scrub |
| 洗心革面 | xǐ xīn gé miàn | turn over a new leaf |
| 洗印 | xǐ yìn | developing and printing; processing |
| 洗澡 | xǐ zǎo | have a bath; bathe |

*Example:*

新 年 到 了 ， 大 家 忙 着 洗 刷 屋 子 和 房 间 。
Xīn nián dào le  dà jiā máng zhe xǐ shuā wū zi hé fáng jiān

Everybody is busy washing and cleaning the house in preparation for the coming new year.

79

**BŌ**

waves;
ripples

The saying goes: "When there is wind in the clouds, there are waves on the river." Such waves (波) appear on the surface and are likened to the skin (皮) of water (氵). When waves (波) of wrinkles appear on the skin of a woman (女), we have 婆 — an old woman.

| | | | | | | | | | | | | | |
|ヽ|冫|氵|氵|汀|沪|波|波| | | | | | |

| 波长 | bō cháng | wavelength | | 波涛 | bō tāo | great waves; billows |
| 波荡 | bō dàng | heave; surge | | 波纹 | bō wén | ripple; corrugation |
| 波段 | bō duàn | wave band | | 波折 | bō zhé | twists and turns |
| 波兰 | Bō Lán | Poland | | 物价波动 | wù jià bō dòng | price fluctuation |
| 波浪 | bō làng | wave | | | | |

*Example:*

事 情 发 生 了 波 折 。
Shì qing fā shēng le bō zhé
Events took an unexpected turn.

80

**HĂI**

sea;
ocean

母 is a picture of a woman with breasts for suckling a child, signifying mother (母).

每 compares a mother ( 母 ) with a sprout ( ㇏ ), always reproducing; hence meaning every, always.

海 represents the sea, where there is always ( 每 ) plenty of water ( シ )

PENG

丶 冫 氵 氵 汇 汇 海 海 海 海

| | | | | |
|---|---|---|---|---|
| 海岸 | hăi àn | coast; seashore | 海枯石烂 | hăi kū shí làn | (even if) the seas run dry and the rocks crumble |
| 海豹 | hăi bào | seal | 海上 | hăi shàng | at sea; on the sea |
| 海滨 | hăi bīn | seaside | 海外 | hăi wài | overseas; abroad |
| 海产 | hăi chăn | marine products | 海湾 | hăi wān | bay; gulf |
| 海盗 | hăi dào | pirate; sea rover | 海峡 | hăi xiá | strait; channel |
| 海港 | hăi găng | seaport; harbour | 海鲜 | hăi xiān | seafood |
| 海关检查 | hăi guān jiăn chá | customs inspection | 海员 | hăi yuán | seaman; sailor; mariner |
| 海军 | hăi jūn | navy | | | |

*Example:*

海 枯 石 烂 心 不 变 。
Hăi  kū  shí  làn  xīn  bù  biàn

The sea may run dry and the rocks may crumble, but our hearts will alway remain loyal.

81

**KĚ** thirsty

The phonetic 曷 is to ask; literally, a beggar (匃) who speaks (曰). 匃 itself means a wanderer (勹) who seeks to enter (入) a refuge (乚). 曰 is a mouth (口) with word (一). When you ask (曷) for water (氵) you must be thirsty: 渴. "When you are thirsty, a drop of water can be likened to a sweet dew."

丶　丶　氵　氵　沪　沪　沪　渇　渇　渇　渇

| | | | |
|---|---|---|---|
| 渴望 | kě wàng | thirst for; long for; yearn for |
| 渴念 | kě niàn | miss very much |
| 渴睡 | kě shuì | a cat nap; to doze; sleepy |
| 渴仰 | kě yǎng | adore; admire |

*Example:*

许 多 青 年 渴 望 参 加 空 军。

Xǔ duō qīng nián kě wàng cān jiā kōng jūn

Many young people long to join the Air Force.

# 法 FǍ

law; statute

Water is essential to life and benefits everybody. Laws are also meant to benefit every citizen. Just as water ( 氵 ) removes ( 去 ) dirt, so the law (法) smoothens morals by removing vices. However, never resort to law; if you win, you lose; and if you lose, you're lost.

丶 丶丶 氵 氵 汁 法 法 法

| | | |
|---|---|---|
| 法案 | fǎ àn | proposed law; bill |
| 法宝 | fǎ bǎo | a magic weapon |
| 法定 | fǎ dìng | legal; statutory |
| 法定人数 | fǎ dìng rén shù | quorum |
| 法官 | fǎ guān | judge; justice |
| 法规 | fǎ guī | laws and regulations |
| 法令 | fǎ lìng | laws and decrees |

| | | |
|---|---|---|
| 法律 | fǎ lǜ | law; statute |
| 法庭 | fǎ tíng | court; tribunal |
| 法网 | fǎ wǎng | the net of justice; the arm of the law |
| 法西斯 | fǎ xī sī | fascist |
| 法子 | fǎ zi | way; method |

*Example:*

我 们 得 想 个 法 子 解 决 这 个 问 题 。

Wǒ men dé xiǎng gè fǎ zi jiě jué zhè ge wèn tí

We'll have to think of a way to solve the problem.

**LÍN**

forest

"A single fibre does not make a thread; a single tree does not make a forest," so goes the saying. The character for tree is a pictograph: 木. Two trees form a company — a grove or forest: 林. Three trees make a crowd, signifying dense or overgrown: 森.

一 十 才 木 林 村 材 林

| 艺林 | yì lín | art circles |
| 竹林 | zhú lín | bamboo grove |
| 林产品 | lín chǎn pǐn | forest products |
| 林带 | lín dài | forest belt |
| 林立 | lín lì | stand in great numbers (like trees in a forest) |
| 林木 | lín mù | forest; woods |
| 林荫道 | lín yīn dào | boulevard; avenue |

*Example:*

港 口 樯 桅 林 立 。

Gǎng kǒu qiáng wéi lín lì

There is a forest of masts in the harbour.

84

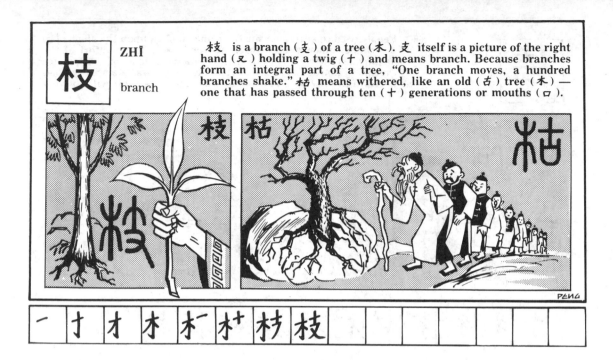

枝 **ZHĪ**

branch

枝 is a branch (支) of a tree (木). 支 itself is a picture of the right hand (又) holding a twig (十) and means branch. Because branches form an integral part of a tree, "One branch moves, a hundred branches shake." 枯 means withered, like an old (古) tree (木) — one that has passed through ten (十) generations or mouths (口).

一 十 才 才 木 术 材 枝

| 枝杈 | zhī chà | branch; twig |
| 枝接 | zhī jiē | scion grafting |
| 枝节 | zhī jié | branches and knots — minor matters; complication; unexpected difficulty |
| 枝叶 | zhī yè | branches and leaves; non-essentials |
| 枝子 | zhī zi | branch; twig |

*Example:*

不 要 过 多 地 注 意 那 些 枝 枝 节 节 。
Bú yào gūo duō de zhù yì nà xiē zhī zhī jié jié

Don't pay too much attention to the minor issues.

85

# 椅 YǏ
chair

People used to sitting on the floor once looked upon the chair (椅) as a strange, unusual (奇) thing of wood (木). The comfort of the chair impelled men (大) to utter exclamations of approval (可); hence 奇, meaning unusual. The sedan chair, however, was a status symbol, as noted in the saying: "The doctor who rides in a chair will not visit the poor."

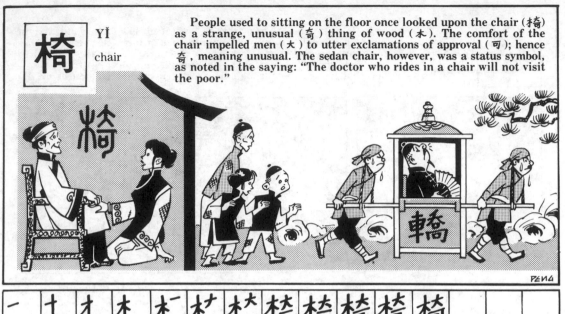

一 十 才 才 木 杧 栌 杺 枋 梌 椅 椅

| | | | |
|---|---|---|---|
| 椅子 | yǐ zi | chair |
| 椅子顶 | yǐ zi dǐng | balancing on a pyramid of chairs |

*Example:*

他 家 很 贫 穷 ， 连 椅 子 也 没 有 。
Tā jiā hěn pín qióng  lián yǐ zi yě méi yǒu
He was so very poor that he had no chairs in his house.

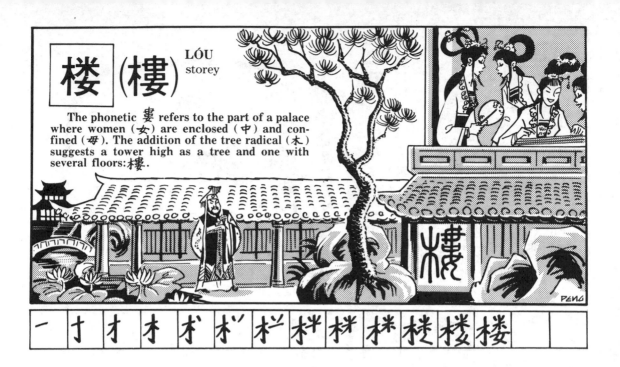

# 楼(樓)

**LÓU**
storey

The phonetic 婁 refers to the part of a palace where women (女) are enclosed (中) and confined (毋). The addition of the tree radical (木) suggests a tower high as a tree and one with several floors: 樓.

一 十 才 才 才 杧 朴 村 村 村 楼 楼 楼

| 楼板 | lóu bǎn | floor; floorslab |
| 楼房 | lóu fáng | a building of two or more storeys |
| 楼上 | lóu shàng | upstairs |
| 楼台 | lóu tái | a high building; tower; balcony |
| 楼梯 | lóu tī | stairs; staircase |
| 楼下 | lóu xià | downstairs |

*Example:*

楼 上 住 的 是 一 位 退 休 老 工 人 。
Lóu shàng zhù de shì yī wèi tuì xiū lǎo gōng rén
A retired worker lives upstairs.

87

病 柄

**BÌNG** sickness

The radical for disease 疒 (疒) is made up of a horizontal line ( − ) — the position of a sick person — and the bed ( 爿 ). The idea of sickness is reinforced by the phonetic 丙 ( 疯 ) — fire ( 火 ) in the house ( 宀 ), referring to high fever. 病 also means defect or fault, and it is said: "A wise doctor never treats himself."

丶 一 广 广 广 疒 疒 病 病 病

| 流行病 | líu xíng bìng | epidemic disease |
| 心脏病 | xīn zàng bìng | heart trouble; heart disease |
| 病从口入 | bìng cóng kǒu rù | illness finds its way in by the mouth |
| 病倒 | bìng dǎo | be down with an illness; be laid up |
| 病假 | bìng jià | sick leave |
| 病况 | bìng kuàng | state of an illness; patient's condition |
| 病态 | bìng tài | morbid state |
| 病痛 | bìng tòng | slight illness; indisposition; ailment |

*Example:*

他 犯 错 误 的 病 根 在 于 私 心 太 重 。

Tā fàn cuò wù de bìng gēn zài yú sī xīn tài zhòng

His error stems from selfishness.

88

**TÉNG**  pain; ache

Just as fire or fever suggests sickness, winter (冬) or intense cold is here combined with the radical for sickness (疒) to signify pain: 疼. However, young and old do not feel pain alike. In youth, the absence of pleasure is pain; in old age, the absence of pain is pleasure.

丶　亠　广　疒　疒　疒　疒　疒　疼　疼

| 疼爱 | téng ài | be very fond of; love dearly |
| 疼痛 | téng tòng | pain; ache; soreness |

*Example:*

婆 婆 最 疼 小 孙 子 。
Pó po zuì téng xiǎo sūn zi
Granny dotes on her little grandson.

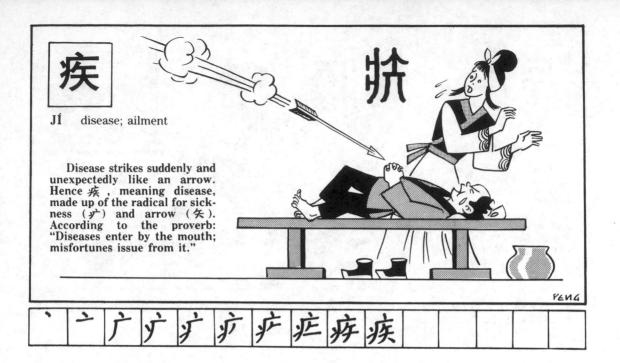

**JÍ**  disease; ailment

Disease strikes suddenly and unexpectedly like an arrow. Hence 疾, meaning disease, made up of the radical for sickness (疒) and arrow (矢). According to the proverb: "Diseases enter by the mouth; misfortunes issue from it."

丶 一 广 广 广 疒 疒 疟 疾 疾

| 眼疾 | yǎn jí | eye trouble |
| 疾病 | jí bìng | disease; illness |
| 疾风 | jí fēng | strong wind; gale |
| 疾苦 | jí kǔ | sufferings; hardships |
| 疾言厉色 | jí yán lì sè | harsh words and stern looks |

*Example:*

他 对 人 很 和 蔼 ， 从 不 疾 言 厉 色 。
Tā duì rén hěn hé ǎi　 cóng bù jí yán lì sè
He is affable and is never brusque with people.

道　DÀO

way; path

首 is a pictograph of a hairy ( ㇀) head ( 百 ) and means head or chief. Combined with 辶 or 辵 (go), it produces 道 — the way of virtue. Head ( 首 ) and feet (辶) advancing on the same path symbolizes the Tao (道), of which it is said: "To believe in the Tao is easy; to keep the Tao is difficult."

丶 丷 丷 䒑 䒑 芐 芐 首 首 首 道 道

| 道德 | dào dé | morals; morality; ethics |
| 道贺 | dào hè | congratulate |
| 道教 | Dào Jiào | Taoism |
| 道具 | dào jù | stage property; prop |
| 道理 | dào li | principle; truth; hows and whys; reason; sense |

| 道路 | dào lù | road; way; path |
| 道歉 | dào qiàn | apologize; make an apology |
| 道士 | dào shi | Taoist priest |
| 道喜 | dào xǐ | congratulate somebody on a happy occasion |
| 道谢 | dào xiè | express one's thanks; thank |

*Example:*

你 的 话 很 有 道 理 。

Nǐ de huà hěn yǒu dào li

What you said is quite reasonable.

91

面　MIÀN

face

This radical incorporates 囗, an outline of the face, with 百 (head) featuring the eyes ( 目 ) as its most prominent part. Because a person is identified by his face, we know a man's face, not his mind. Nevertheless, "Be able to say in his face what you say behind his back."

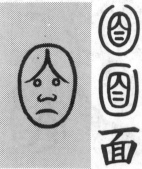

一 ｢ 丆 丙 而 而 面 面

| 面对 | miàn duì | face; confront |
| 面对面 | miàn duì miàn | facing each other; face-to-face |
| 面粉 | miàn fěn | wheat flour; flour |
| 面红耳赤 | miàn hóng ěr chì | be flushed |
| 面积 | miàn ji | area |
| 面颊 | miàn jiá | cheek |

| 面具 | miàn jù | mask |
| 面貌 | miàn mào | face; features |
| 面目 | miàn mù | face; features; look; aspect |
| 面前 | miàn qián | in front of; before |
| 面熟 | mià shú | look familiar |
| 面条 | miàn tiáo | noodles |
| 面子 | miàn zi | reputation; prestige; face |

*Example:*

展 览 会 面 积 为 三 千 平 方 米 。

Zhǎn lǎn huì miàn ji wéi sān qiān píng fāng mǐ

The exhibition covers a floor space of 3000 square metres.

92

瞎

**XIĀ**   blind

瞎害 stands for injured (害) eyes (目).
The phonetic 害 (harm) represents
injury from a stick ( 丨 ) with notches
( 三 ) or injury by mouth ( 口 ) under
cover ( 宀 ).

Another ideograph for blind is 盲
or lost ( 亡 ) eyes ( 目 ). Despite their
handicap, "The blind are quick at
hearing; the deaf are quick at sight."

丨 冂 冂 月 目 目` 目' 目宀 目宀 目宀 目宀 睅 睎 睛 瞎

| | | |
|---|---|---|
| 瞎扯 | xiā chě | talk irresponsibly; talk rubbish |
| 瞎话 | xiā huà | untruth; lie |
| 瞎闹 | xiā nào | act senselessly; mess about; fool around; be mischievous |
| 瞎说 | xiā shuō | talk irresponsibly; talk rubbish |
| 瞎子 | xiā zi | a blind person |

*Example:*

赶 快 做 作 业 ， 别 瞎 闹 。
Gǎn kuài zuò zuò yè　　bié xiā nào
Do your homework quickly and don't fool around.

93

## 睡

**SHUÌ**

sleep

睡 is to have the eyes or eyelids ( 目 ) hanging down ( 垂 ) — to sleep. The phonetic 垂 or 坙 depicts a bough loaded with leaves (㐅) hanging down towards the earth ( 土 ). Sleep, even if your eyes are closed, is not always a peaceful affair. According to the saying, "Attending to the Emperor is like sleeping with a tiger."

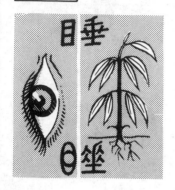

| 睡觉 | shuì jiào | sleep |
| 睡莲 | shuì lián | water lily |
| 睡梦 | shuì mèng | sleep; slumber |
| 睡眠 | shuì mián | sleep |
| 睡醒 | shuì xǐng | wake up |
| 睡衣 | shuì yī | night clothes; pyjamas |
| 睡意 | shuì yì | sleepiness; drowsiness |

*Example:*

一 阵 敲 门 声 把 他 从 睡 梦 中 惊 醒 了 。

Yī zhèn qiāo mén shēng bǎ tā cóng shuì mèng zhōng jīng xǐng le

He was roused from sleep by a heavy pounding on the door.

94

# 发 （髮）

**FÀ**  hair

The seal form of the radical 髟 is 彩. It depicts long hair ( 丂 ) tied with a band ( 一 ) and pinned with a brooch ( 丫 ). Three strokes are added to emphasize the locks ( 彡 ). The phonetic 发 or 犮 is a dog led by a leash — an allusion to the practice of leading underdogs by the hair.

乚 𠂇 发 发 发

| | | | |
|---|---|---|---|
| 理发 | lǐ fà | haircut |
| 发型 | fà xíng | hair style; hairdo |
| 发表 | fā biǎo | publish; issue |
| 发财 | fā cái | get rich; make a fortune |
| 发愁 | fā chóu | worry; be anxious |
| 发达 | fā dá | developed; flourishing |
| 发动 | fā dòng | start; launch; mobilize |
| 发抖 | fā dǒu | shiver; shake; tremble |

| | | |
|---|---|---|
| 发愤 | fā fèn | make a firm resolution |
| 发慌 | fā huāng | feel nervous; get flustered |
| 发觉 | fā jué | find; detect; discover |
| 发明 | fā míng | invent |
| 发生 | fā shēng | happen; occur; take place |
| 发售 | fā shòu | sell; put on sale |
| 发言权 | fā yán quán | right to speak |
| 发展 | fā zhǎn | develop; expand; grow |

*Example:*

那 里 发 生 了 强 烈 地 震 。
Nà  li  fā  shēng  le  qiáng  liè  dì  zhèn
A violent earthquake occurred there.

95

胃

**WÈI**　stomach

This ideograph combines two pictographs. The upper one is a pouch filled with rice: ⊗ ; the lower, a piece of flesh: 月 . Hence, stomach — a fleshy pouch filled with rice. Although a full stomach begets a contented mind, "Better be hungry and pure than well-filled and corrupt."

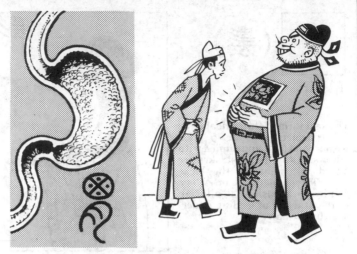

丶 冂 冃 冄 田 胃 胃 胃 胃

| 胃病 | wèi bìng | stomach trouble; gastric disease |
| 胃口 | wèi kǒu | appetite; liking |
| 胃溃疡 | wèi kuì yáng | gastric ulcer |
| 胃酸 | wèi suān | hydrochloric acid in gastric juice |
| 胃痛 | wèi tòng | gastralgia |
| 胃液 | wèi yè | gastric juice |

*Example:*

她 的 胃 口 很 好 ， 吃 了 很 多 。
Tā　de　wèi　kǒu　hěn　hǎo　　chī　le　hěn　duō
She was eating a lot because she had a very good appetite.

96

**SĪ** think

This ideograph combines the skull (⊗) with the heart (心) to produce thought: 思. The faculties of reasoning and feeling are here exercised to create a balanced mind. And, according to the saying, "If you wish to know the mind of a man, listen to his words."

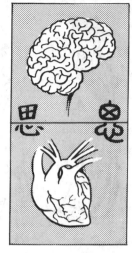

PENG

| 丶 | 冂 | 𠃌 | 甶 | 田 | 甶 | 思 | 思 | 思 |

| 思潮 | sī cháo | trend of thought; ideological trend; thoughts |
| 思考 | sī kǎo | think deeply; ponder over; reflect on |
| 思念 | sī niàn | think of; long for; miss |
| 思索 | sī suǒ | think deeply; ponder |
| 思想 | sī xiǎng | thought; thinking; idea; ideology |

*Example:*

我 一 夜 没 睡 着 ， 反 复 思 索 这 个 问 题 。
Wǒ yī yè méi shuì zháo fǎn fù sī suǒ zhè ge wèn tí
I lay awake all night, turning the problem over and over in my mind.

97

# 情 QÍNG

feeling;
affection

青 is green — the colour (丹) of nature and growing plants (生). With the addition of the radical for heart (忄) the character stands for those feelings which are pure or natural to the heart of man: 情. Lamenting the lack of depth and substance in such feelings, the saying goes: "Human feelings are as thin as sheets of paper."

PENG

丶 丷 忄 忄一 忄二 忖 性 情 情 情 情

| 情报 | qíng bào | intelligence; information |
| 情不自禁 | qíng bù zì jìn | be seized with a sudden impulse to |
| 情操 | qíng cāo | sentiment |
| 情敌 | qíng dí | rival in love |
| 情调 | qíng diào | sentiment; emotional appeal |
| 情窦初开 | qíng dòu chū kāi | (of a young girl) first awakening of love |
| 情感 | qíng gǎn | emotion; feeling |

| 情节 | qíng jié | plot; circumstances |
| 情况 | qíng kuàng | circumstances; situation |
| 情理 | qíng lǐ | reason; sense |
| 情侣 | qíng lǚ | sweethearts; lovers |
| 情趣 | qíng qù | temperament and interest |
| 情绪 | qíng xù | morale; feeling; mood; sentiments |
| 情愿 | qíng yuàn | be willing to; would rather |

*Example:*

这 个 剧 本 情 节 很 复 杂 。
Zhè ge jù běn qíng jié hěn fù zá
The play has a very complicated plot.

# 拜 BÀI

salute
respect;

拜, to pay respects to man or god, was first written as 𢕱, depicting two hands (𢦏) hanging down (下 or 丅) in salutation or worship. With respect to worship, it has been said: "He who lives near the temple ridicules the gods." Also: "Far better it is to be respectful at home than to burn incense in a far place."

| 拜别 | bài bié | take leave of |
|------|---------|---------------|
| 拜倒 | bài dǎo | prostrate oneself; fall on one's knees |
| 拜访 | bài fǎng | pay a visit |
| 拜见 | bài jiàn | pay a formal visit; call to pay respects |
| 拜年 | bài nián | pay a New Year call |
| 拜寿 | bài shòu | congratulate an elderly person on his birthday |
| 拜托 | bài tuō | request somebody to do something |

*Example:*

姑 妈 ， 我 们 给 您 拜 年 来 啦 ！
Gū mā wǒ men gěi nín bài nián lái la

Auntie, we've come to wish you a Happy New Year.

99

**FÀNG**

release

放 means to release — to drive out (攴) into an open space or pasture (方). The radical 攴 (攵) is a hand with stick; the phonetic 方 is a square or open space. Horses or cattle released for grazing can always be rounded up, but "Words once released cannot be recaptured by the swiftest steeds."

丶 亠 亣 方 方 疒 扩 放

| | | |
|---|---|---|
| 放出 | fàng chū | give out; let out; emit |
| 放大 | fàng dà | enlarge; magnify; amplify |
| 放胆 | fàng dǎn | act boldly and with confidence |
| 放荡 | fàng dàng | dissolute; dissipated |
| 放工 | fàng gōng | (of workers) knock off |
| 放火 | fàng huǒ | set fire to; set on fire |
| 放假 | fàng jià | have a vacation; have a day off |
| 放宽 | fàng kuān | relax restrictions; relax |

| | | |
|---|---|---|
| 放弃 | fàng qì | abandon; give up; renounce |
| 放下 | fàng xià | lay down; put down |
| 放心 | fàng xīn | set one's mind at rest |
| 放学 | fàng xué | classes are over |
| 放映 | fàng yìng | show; project |
| 放置 | fàng zhì | lay up; lay aside |
| 放逐 | fàng zhú | send into exile; banish |

*Example:*

你 放 心 ， 一 切 都 会 安 排 好 的 。

Nǐ fàng xīn yī qiè dōu huì ān pái hǎo de

You can rest assured that everything will be all right.

100

ZHÈNG

government

The radical 攴 represents the right hand wielding the rod of authority. The phonetic 正 signifies a foot (止) walking the straight way (一). Hence 政 which means government, an upright (正) administration (攴) — an enforcement for good. No wonder the saying goes: "Beasts hate the net as people dislike government."

一　丁　下　正　正　正　政　政

| 政变 | zhèng biàn | coup d'etat | 政界 | zhèng jiè | political circles; government circles |
| 政策 | zhèng cè | policy | 政局 | zhèng jú | political situation; political scene |
| 政党 | zhèng dǎng | political party | 政客 | zhèng kè | politician |
| 政敌 | zhèng dí | political opponent | 政权 | zhèng quán | political power; regime |
| 政法 | zhèng fǎ | politics and law | 政治 | zhèng zhì | politics; political affairs |
| 政府 | zhèng fǔ | government | | | |

*Example:*

哥　哥　在　政　府　部　门　工　作　。

Gē　ge　zài　zhèng　fǔ　bù　mén　gōng　zuō

My elder brother works in the civil service.

**CÀI**

vegetable

菜, the character for vegetables, is made up of 艹 and 采. The radical for grass ( 艹 ) suggests a small plant. 采, the phonetic, shows the right hand ( ⺕ ) reaching down to pluck the fruit of a plant or tree ( 木 ). How often we have plucked such fruit, thinking nothing of the tree that bore it and the One who made it grow!

一 十 卄 艹 艹 芋 芈 苹 苹 芧 菜

| 菜场 | cài chǎng | food market |
| 菜单 | cài dān | menu |
| 菜花 | cài huā | cauliflower |
| 菜农 | cài nóng | vegetable grower |
| 菜市 | cài shì | food market |
| 菜蔬 | cài shū | vegetables |
| 菜园 | cài yuán | vegetable garden; vegetable farm |

*Example:*

舅 母 的 家 后 面 有 一 小 片 菜 园 。

Jiù  mǔ  de  jiā  hòu mian yǒu  yī  xiǎo piān  cài  yuán

My aunt has a small plot of vegetable garden at the back of her house.

**TIÁN**

sweet;
pleasant

舌 shows the tongue (千) in the mouth (口). 甘 depicts something (一) worth holding in the mouth (口). So 甜 means sweet (甘) to the tongue (舌). However, beware of anything sweet from the tongue, for the tongue is like a sharp knife that kills without drawing blood. Hence the proverb: "Bitter words are medicine; sweet words bring illness."

PENG

丿 二 千 千 舌 舌 舌 甜 甜 甜 甜

| | | | | |
|---|---|---|---|---|

甜美　　　tián měi　　　sweet; luscious; pleasant; refreshing

甜蜜　　　tiái mì　　　sweet; happy

甜品　　　tiái pǐn　　　sweetmeats

甜头　　　tián tou　　　sweet taste; pleasant flavour; good benefit (as an inducement)

甜味　　　tián wèi　　　sweet taste

甜言蜜语　tián yán mì yǔ　sweet words and honeyed phrases; fine-sounding words

*Example:*

这　西　瓜　好　甜　哪 !
Zhè　xǐ　guā　hǎo　tián　na
This watermelon is really sweet!

103

叫 JIÀO

call

叫 is to call out (口) the measure (斗). The ancient form of 斗 depicts a measuring ladle (ㄅ) with ten (十): 斗. Although vendors shout out their wares, a melon seller never cries "Bitter melons!" nor a wine seller "Thin wine!"

| 叫喊 | jiào hǎn | shout; yell; howl |
| 叫好 | jiào hǎo | applaud |
| 叫唤 | jiào huan | cry out; call out |
| 叫苦 | jiào kǔ | complain of hardship or suffering; moan and groan |
| 叫骂 | jiào mà | shout curses |
| 叫门 | jiào mén | call at the door to be let in |
| 叫醒 | jiào xǐng | wake up; awaken |
| 叫座 | jiào zuò | draw a large audience; draw well; appeal to the audience |

*Example:*

外边有人叫你。

Wài biān yǒu rén jiào nǐ

Somebody outside is calling you.

# 听 (聽)

**TĪNG**    hear; listen

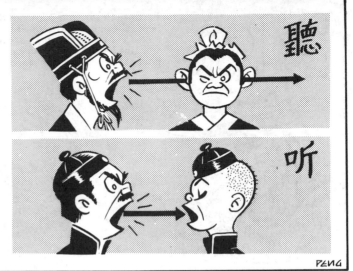

聽 is the rectification (直 or 㤞) of the heart (心) of a listener or disciple (壬) by his ear (耳); hence to listen or obey. The simplified form 听 combines 口 (mouth) with 斤 (discerning), i.e., to discern what comes from the mouth — by listening. It may even suggest that most people today listen with their mouths!

| 一 | 冂 | 口 | 口ノ | 叮 | 吓 | 听 | | | | | | | |

| | | |
|---|---|---|
| 听从 | tīng cóng | obey; heed; comply with |
| 听而不闻 | tīng ér bù wén | hear but pay no attention |
| 听话 | tīng huà | be obedient |
| 听觉 | tīng jué | sense of hearing |
| 听说 | tīng shuō | be told; hear of |
| 听筒 | tīng tǒng | (telephone) receiver; headphone; earphone |
| 听写 | tīng xiě | dictation |
| 听众 | tīng zhòng | audience; listeners |

*Example:*

我 们 从 来 没 听 说 过 这 种 事 。
Wǒ men cóng lái méi tīng shuō gūo zhè zhǒng shì

We've never heard of such a thing.

105

# 聋（聾）
## LÓNG deaf

Because the dragon is king of the supernatural creatures (the others being the unicorn, the phoenix and the tortoise), it can afford to turn a deaf ear to anything. Hence dragon's (龙) ear (耳), meaning deaf: 聋. But let not those who cannot hear well lose heart: "In the kingdom of the deaf, the one-eared man is king!"

| 一 | 十 | 尤 | 龙 | 龙 | 龙 | 龙 | 龙 | 聋 | 聋 | 聋 | | | |

聋哑　　　lóng yǎ　　　deaf and dumb; deaf-mute
聋子　　　lóng zi　　　a deaf person

*Example:*

她 在 一 间 聋 哑 学 校 当 教 员 。
Tā zài yì jiān lóng yǎ xué xiào dāng jiào yuán
She works as a teacher in the school for deaf-mutes.

106

# 喜

**xǐ**

happiness;
pleasure

喜 or happiness is expressed by 壴 (music) and 口 (singing). 壴 depicts the ancient drum on its stand (豆) with its stretched skin (一) and a straightened right hand (屮) striking it. 口 represents the mouth singing. True happiness, however, comes from unselfish giving; and when you make two people happy, one of them is probably you.

PENG

| 一 | 十 | 士 | 声 | 吉 | 吉 | 直 | 直 | 喜 | 喜 | 喜 | 喜 | | |

| 喜爱 | xǐ ài | like; love; be fond of; be keen on |
| 喜欢 | xǐ huan | like; love; happy; elated; filled with joy |
| 喜酒 | xǐ jiǔ | wedding feast |
| 喜剧 | xǐ jù | comedy |
| 喜怒无常 | xǐ nù wú cháng | subject to changing moods |
| 喜气洋洋 | xǐ qì yáng yáng | full of joy; jubilant |
| 喜事 | xǐ shì | happy event; wedding |
| 喜新厌旧 | xǐ xīn yàn jiù | love the new and loathe the old — be fickle in affection |

*Example:*

这 孩 子 真 讨 人 喜 欢 。
Zhè hái zi zhēn tǎo rén xǐ huan

This is a lovable child.

107

# CHŪN

## 春

### spring

, the seal character for spring (春), signifies the growth and outburst (屯) of vegetation (屮屮) under the influence of the sun (日). As unpredictable and changeable as the weather, spring comes either early or late each year. Hence the proverb: "Spring has a stepmother's face."

一 二 三 丰 夫 表 春 春 春

| 春风满面 | chūn fēng mǎn miàn | beaming with satisfaction; radiant with happiness |
| 春光 | chūn guāng | sights and sounds of spring |
| 春季 | chūn jì | spring; springtime |
| 春卷 | chūn juǎn | spring roll |
| 春联 | chūn lián | Spring Festival couplets (pasted on gateposts or door panels); New Year scrolls |
| 春秋 | chūn qiū | spring and autumn; year; the Spring and Autumn Period (770-476 B.C.) |
| 春天 | chūn tiān | spring; springtime |

*Example:*

看 他 春 风 满 面 ， 一 定 有 好 消 息 告 诉 我 们 。
Kàn tā chūn fēng mǎn miàn yí dìng yǒu hǎo xiāo xi gào su wǒ men

His face is beaming with happiness; he must have some good news for us.

**CHÀNG**   sing

昌 is composed of 日 (sun) and 曰 (speak). 曰 is the mouth ( 口 ) that exhales a breath; by extension, exhalation and emanation. So 昌 means prosperous or splendid, just as the sun sends forth rays and the mouth puts forth words.

唱 therefore refers to singing which produces a more refined quality of the voice than an ordinary conversation.

| 唱词 | chàng cí | libretto; words of a ballad |
| 唱歌 | chàng gē | sing (a song) |
| 唱工 | chàng gōng | art of singing; singing |
| 唱片 | chàng piàn | gramophone record |
| 唱诗班 | chàng shī bān | choir |
| 电唱机 | diàn chàng jī | record player |

*Example:*

她 很 会 唱 歌 。
Tā hěn huì chàng gē
She is a good singer.

**GĒ**

歌

song

可 is an exclamation of approval ( 丁 ) from the mouth ( 口 ) and means can or may.

哥 is 可 doubled, suggesting singing, now used for addressing elder brother by sound loan.

歌 adds breath ( 欠 ) to singing ( 哥 ) to produce a song.

一 厂 丌 可 可 可 叮 哥 哥 哥 哥 歌 歌 歌

| | | | |
|---|---|---|---|
| 歌本 | gē běn | songbook | |
| 歌词 | gē cí | words of a song | |
| 歌功颂德 | gē gōng sòng dé | eulogize somebody's virtues and achievements | |
| 歌喉 | gē hóu | (singer's) voice | |
| 歌剧 | gē jù | opera | |
| 歌谱 | gē pǔ | music of a song | |

| | | |
|---|---|---|
| 歌曲 | gē qǔ | song |
| 歌手 | gē shǒu | singer; vocalist |
| 歌颂 | gē sòng | sing the praises of |
| 歌舞 | gē wǔ | song and dance |
| 歌谣 | gē yáo | ballad; folk song; nursery rhyme |
| 歌咏比赛 | gē yǒng bǐ sài | singing contest |

*Example:*

这 首 歌 的 歌 词 很 动 人 。

Zhè shǒu gē de gē cí hěn dòng rén

The words of this song are most touching.

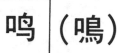

**鸣（鳴）**

**MÍNG**    cry of bird,
animal or insect

Because a bird (鸟) chirps
or sings with its mouth ( 口 ),
we have the character 鸣
applied to the cry of birds,
animals or insects. Some-
times even man crows — like
the rooster that thinks the
sun rises to hear him crow.

PENG

| 丶 | 冂 | 口 | 叮 | 叽 | 吩 | 鸣 | 鸣 | | | | | | |
|---|---|---|---|---|---|---|---|---|---|---|---|---|---|

| 鸡鸣 | jī míng | the crow of a cock |
|---|---|---|
| 鸣谢 | míng xiè | express one's thanks formally |
| 鸣放 | míng fàng | airing of views |
| 鸣锣开道 | míng luó kāi dào | beat gongs to clear the way (for officials in feudal times); |
| | | prepare the public for a coming event |
| 鸣禽 | míng qín | songbird; singing bird |
| 鸣冤叫屈 | míng yuān jiào qū | complain and call for redress; voice grievances |

*Example:*

钟 鸣 三 下 。

Zhōng míng sān xià

The clock struck three.

111

吐

TŬ   spit out
TÙ   vomit

The ideograph 吐, literally from mouth ( 口 ) to earth ( 土 ), means to spit or vomit. Figuratively, it means to disclose or reveal the truth — like spilling the beans or letting the cat out of the bag. In this sense, beware: "A very big secret can be vomited out of a little mouth."

| 丶 | 丿 | 口 | 口 | 吐 | 吐 |

| 吐露 | tǔ lù | reveal; tell |
| 吐气 | tǔ qì | feel elated after unburdening oneself of resentment |
| 吐沫 | tù mo | saliva; spittle; spit |
| 吐血 | tù xiě | spitting blood; haematemesis |
| 吐泻 | tù xiè | vomitting and diarrhoea |

*Example:*

他 不 愿 意 吐 露 真 情 。
Tā bú yuàn yì tǔ lù zhēn qíng

He was reluctant to reveal the truth.

## 如 RÚ

like; as

Ideographically, 如 is to speak (口) like or as a woman (女), that is, appropriately to the circumstances and the disposition of the man she desires to influence. Testifying to such persuasive, womanly skill is the saying: "The walls of a city are raised by men's wisdom but overthrown by women's wiles."

PENG

| 如常 | rú cháng | as usual |
| 如此 | rú cǐ | so; such; in this way |
| 如此而已 | rú cǐ ér yǐ | that's what it all adds up to |
| 如果 | rú guǒ | if; in case; in the event of |
| 如何 | rú hé | how; what |
| 如今 | rú jīn | nowadays; now |
| 如期 | rú qī | as scheduled; on schedule |

| 如意 | rú yì | as one wishes |
| 如意算盘 | rú yì suàn pan | wishful thinking |
| 如鱼得水 | rú yú dé shuǐ | feel just like fish in water; be in one's element |
| 如愿以偿 | rú yuàn yǐ cháng | have one's wish fulfilled; achieve what one wishes |

*Example:*

会 议 将 如 期 召 开 。

Huì yì jiāng rú qī zhào kāi

The conference will be convened as scheduled.

## 娘 NÍANG

mother; young mother

The modern form 娘 signifies a woman (女) who is virtuous and respectable (良) — a good woman, a mother or a young woman.

The old form 孃 stands for a homely and helpful (襄) woman (女). Of such a woman it is said: "The homely woman is precious in the home, but at a feast the beautiful one is preferred."

ㄥ ㄥ 女 女 女 女 女 娘 娘 娘

| 新娘 | xin níang | bride |
| 娘家 | níang jia | a married woman's parents' home |
| 娘娘 | níang niang | empress or imperial concubine of the first rank; goddess |
| 娘胎 | niǎng tāi | mother's womb |

*Example:*

嫂 嫂 回 娘 家 去 了 。

Sǎo sao huí níang jia qù le

My sister-in-low has gone to visit her parents.

**MIÀO**

妙

wonderful

At 17 or 18 there are no ugly girls. So the characters 少 (young) and 女 (woman) together form the ideograph 妙, an adjective of admiration meaning wonderful, excellent and beautiful. Notwithstanding this, "Ugly wives and stupid servant girls are treasures above price."

| 妙不可言 | miào bù kě yán | too wonderful for words; most intriguing |
| 妙计 | miào jì | excellent plan; brilliant scheme |
| 妙诀 | miào jué | a clever way of doing something; knack |
| 妙趣横生 | miào qù héng shēng | full of wit and humour; very witty |
| 妙手回春 | miào shǒu huí chūn | (of a doctor) effect a miraculous cure and bring the dying back to life |
| 妙用 | miào yòng | magical effect |
| 妙语 | miào yǔ | witty remark; witticism |

*Example:*

他　回　答　得　很　妙　。

Tā　huí　dá　dé　hěn　miào

He made a clever answer.

# 客

**KÈ**

guest;
visitor

夂 represents a man following his own way.
各 signifies his going his way ( 夂 ) without heeding advice ( 口 ); by extension, each or every.
客 is a guest — one who has his way under another's roof ( 宀 ). No wonder "the host is happy when the guest is gone."

、 丶 宀 宀 宀 容 宓 客 客

| | | | |
|---|---|---|---|
| 客船 | kè chuán | passenger ship | |
| 客串 | kè chuàn | be a guest performer | |
| 客队 | kè duì | (sports) visiting team | |
| 客房 | kè fáng | guest room | |
| 客观 | kè guān | objective | |
| 客机 | kè jī | passenger plane; airliner | |

| | | |
|---|---|---|
| 客满 | kè mǎn | (of theatre tickets, etc.) sold out; full house |
| 客气 | kè qi | polite; courteous; dest |
| 客人 | kè rén | visitor; guest |
| 客套 | kè tào | polite formula; civilities |

*Example:*

他 对 人 很 客 气 。
Tā  duì  rén  hěn  kè  qi
He is very polite to people.

## 比 BǏ

compare

The seal form of 比 reveals this character as an inverted form of 从 (follow). It represents two men standing as if to compare heights. "When compared with those above," so goes the saying, "there is something lacking; but compared with those below, there is something to spare."

一 匕 比 比

| 比方 | bǐ fang | analogy; instance |
| 比分 | bǐ fēn | score |
| 比价 | bǐ jià | price relations; parity; rate of exchange |
| 比较 | bǐ jiào | compare; contrast; fairly; comparatively; quite; rather |
| 比率 | bǐ lǜ | ratio; rate |
| 比如 | bǐ rú | for example; for instance |
| 比赛 | bǐ sài | match; competition |
| 比喻 | bǐ yù | metaphor; analogy |

*Example:*

这 只 是 一 个 比 喻 的 说 法 。
Zhè zhǐ shì yī ge bǐ yù de shuō fa

This is just a figure of speech.

117

| 背 | **BĒI**<br>back; oppose<br><br>**BĒI**<br>carry on the<br>back | A person sitting facing the south (as is the custom) and back to back with another suggests north: 北. Turning one's back on another signifies opposition. Hence 背, referring to the back (北) of the body (月), may mean to oppose or to carry on the back. |
| --- | --- | --- |

PENG

| 丨 | 一 | 丬 | 才 | 北 | 北<br>丿 | 背<br>刀 | 背<br>月 | 背<br>月 | | | |

| 背痛 | bèi tòng | backache |
| --- | --- | --- |
| 背地里 | bèi dì li | behind somebody's back; privately; on the sly |
| 背后 | bèi hòu | behind; at the back; in the rear |
| 背脊 | bèi ji | the back of the human body |
| 背井离乡 | bèi jǐng lí xiāng | leave one's native place (especially against one's will) |
| 背景 | bèi jǐng | background; backdrop |
| 背叛 | bèi pàn | betray; forsake |
| 背诵 | bèi sòng | recite; repeat from memory |

*Example:*

我 怕 背 不 起 这 样 的 责 任 。
Wǒ pà bēi bù qǐ zhè yàng de zé rèn
I'm afraid I can't shoulder such a responsibility

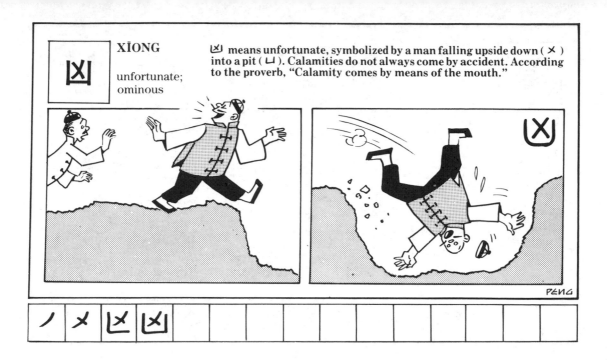

**XIŌNG**

unfortunate;
ominous

凶 means unfortunate, symbolized by a man falling upside down ( ✕ ) into a pit ( ㄩ ). Calamities do not always come by accident. According to the proverb, "Calamity comes by means of the mouth."

| 凶残 | xiōng cán | fierce and cruel; savage and cruel |
| 凶多吉少 | xiōng duō jí shǎo | bode ill rather than well; be fraught with grim possibilities |
| 凶恶 | xiōng è | fierce, ferocious; fiendish |
| 凶犯 | xiōng fàn | one who has committed homicide; murderer |
| 凶猛 | xiōng měng | violent; ferocious |
| 凶器 | xiōng qì | tool or weapon for criminal purposes; lethal weapon |
| 凶杀 | xiōng shā | homicide; murder |
| 凶手 | xiōng shǒu | murderer; assassin; assailant |

*Example:*

这 个 人 样 子 真 凶 。
Zhè ge rén yàng zi zhēn xiōng
This chap looks really fierce.

119

# 答

**DÁ**   reply; answer

Because of its beauty, design and harmony (合), the bamboo (竹) is used here as a perfect example of an answer or reply: 答. However, like bamboos, answers come in various lengths. Many a short question is evaded by a long answer.

| 答非所问 | dá fēi suǒ wèn | an irrelevent answer |
| 答案 | dá àn | answer; solution; key |
| 答辩 | dá biàn | reply (to a charge, query or an argument) |
| 答词 | dá cí | thank-you speech; answering speech; reply |
| 答复 | dá fù | answer; reply |
| 答谢 | dá xiè | express appreciation; acknowledge |
| 答应 | dá yìng | answer; respond; agree; promise; comply with |

*Example:*

你 怎 么 不 答 话 ?
Nǐ  zěn  me  bù  dá  huà

Why don't you answer?

120

# 篮 (籃)

**LÁN**  basket

監 is to bend over (臥) a full vase (皿) to examine its contents; by extension, to oversee those who are confined in a prison. When the bamboo radical 竹 is added, we have a bamboo container to confine goods for safe transportation — a basket: 籃, now simplified to 篮.

PENG

| 丿 | 𠂉 | 𠂢 | 𥫗 | 𥫗 | 竹 | 𥫗 | 𥫗 | 𥫗 | 筱 | 筱 | 笁 | 筥 | 篮 | 篮 |
|---|---|---|---|---|---|---|---|---|---|---|---|---|---|---|

| 投篮 | tóu lán | (basketball) shoot a basket |
| 篮球 | lán qiú | basketball |
| 篮圈 | lán quān | (basketball) ring; hoop |
| 篮子 | lán zi | basket |

*Example:*

今 天 学 校 举 行 了 一 场 篮 球 比 赛 。

Jīn tiān xué xiào jǔ xíng le yī chǎng lán qiú bǐ sài

A basketball match was held in the school today.

## 井 JǏNG well

Originally the seal form 丼 represented fields divided among eight families, with the well in the middle plot to serve the public. The well also serves to expose man's inclination to faultfinding: "One does not blame the shortness of the rope, but the deepness of the well."

一 二 丰 井

| 矿井 | kuàng jǐng | pit; mine |
| 油井 | yóu jǐng | oil well; neat; orderly |
| 井场 | jǐng cháng | well site |
| 井底之蛙 | jǐng dǐ zhī wā | a frog in a well — a person with a very limited outlook |
| 井架 | jǐng jià | derrick |
| 井井有条 | jǐng jǐng yǒu tiáo | in perfect order; shipshape; methodical |
| 井水不犯河水 | jǐng shuǐ bú fàn hé shuǐ | well water does not intrude into river water — I'll mind my own business, you mind yours |

*Example:*

各 种 仪 器 、 工 具 摆 得 井 井 有 条 。
Gè zhǒng yí qì gōng jù bǎi de jǐng jǐng yǒu tiáo
All the instruments and tools are kept in perfect order.

122

石 **SHÍ**

stone

石 is a picture of a piece of stone or rock ( 口 ) falling from a cliff ( 厂 ).

岩 is a steep rock ( 石 ) or cliff that looks like a hill ( 山 ). The rock, being strong, symbolizes integrity. Hence: "Slander cannot destroy an honest man; when the flood recedes the rock appears."

一 丁 丆 石 石

| | | | |
|---|---|---|---|
| 石斑鱼 | shí bān yú | grouper | |
| 石壁 | shí bì | cliff; precipice | |
| 石沉大海 | shí chén dà hǎi | like a stone dropped into the sea — disappear forever | |
| 石雕 | shí diāo | stone carving; carved stone | |
| 石膏 | shí gāo | gypsum; plaster stone | |
| 石工 | shígōng | masonry; stonemason; mason | |

| | | |
|---|---|---|
| 石灰 | shí huī | lime |
| 石榴 | shí liu | pomegranate |
| 石头 | shí tou | stone; rock |
| 石印 | shí yìn | lithographic printing; lithography |
| 石英 | shí yīng | quartz |
| 石油 | shí yóu | petroleum; oil |
| 石子 | shí zi | cobblestone; cobble; pebble |

*Example:*

这 块 石 头 是 从 山 上 拾 回 来 的 。

Zhè kuài shí tou shì cóng shān shàng shí huí lai de

This stone was picked up from the mountain.

仙

XIAN

fairy;
recluse

The ancient form 僊 signifies
a human (人) who rises by
climbing with his head (囟) and
four hands (𦥑), probably
after the manner of a monkey.
An official seal (㔾) is added
to denote promotion. The
modern form 仙 associates
person (亻) with mountain
(山), suggesting recluse and
fairy.

| ノ | 亻 | 亻l | 仙 | 仙 | | | | | | | | | |
|---|---|---|---|---|---|---|---|---|---|---|---|---|---|

| 仙丹 | xiān dān | elixir of life |
|---|---|---|
| 仙姑 | xiāng gū | female immortal; sorceress |
| 仙鹤 | xiān hè | red-crowned crane |
| 仙境 | xiān jìng | fairyland; wonderland; paradise |
| 仙女 | xiān nǚ | female celestial; fairy maiden |
| 仙人掌 | xiān rén zhǎng | cactus |

*Example:*

这 棵 仙 人 掌 有 很 多 刺 。
Zhè  kē  xiān rén zhǎng yǒu hěn duō  cì

This cactus is covered with prickles.

124

**GĀO**

high; tall

高 is a pictograph of a high tower or pavilion ( 占 ) on a lofty sub-structure ( 冂 ) equipped with a hall ( 口 ). It stands for high. When it comes to position, no person stoops so low as the one most eager to rise high in the world. But beware: "He who climbs too high will have a heavy fall."

`丶　一　亠　𠁣　古　亠　高　高　高　高`

| | | | |
|---|---|---|---|
| 高傲 | gāo ào | supercilious; arrogant | |
| 高超音速 | gāo chāo yīn sù | hypersonic speed | |
| 高潮 | gāo cháo | high tide; upsurge; climax | |
| 高大 | gāo dà | tall and big; tall | |
| 高度 | gāo dù | altitude; height | |
| 高峰 | gāo fēng | peak; summit; height | |
| 高贵 | gāo guì | noble; high; elitist | |

| | | |
|---|---|---|
| 高级 | gāo jí | senior; high-ranking |
| 高见 | gāo jiàn | your brilliant idea |
| 高举 | gāo jǔ | hold high; hold aloft |
| 高烧 | gāo shāo | high fever |
| 高兴 | gāo xìng | glad; happy; cheerful |
| 高血压 | gāo xuè yā | hypertension |
| 高原 | gāo yuán | plateau; highland |

*Example:*

你 不 高 兴 去 就 甭 去 了 。
Nǐ bù gāo xìng qù jiù béng qù le
You needn't go if you don't feel like it.

**JĪNG**

capital city

京 is derived from 高 (high). It is a contraction of 高 with the lower part replaced by 小 , a pivot, conveying the idea of loftiness and centrality. So lofty is the capital city that it is said: "One who can speak, speaks of the city; one who cannot, talks merely of household affairs."

| 丶 | 一 | 宀 | 亠 | 古 | 宁 | 京 | 京 | | | | | | |
|---|---|---|---|---|---|---|---|---|---|---|---|---|---|

京城      jīng chéng      the capital of a country
京剧      jīng jù      Beijing opera

*Example:*

妈 妈 最 喜 欢 看 京 剧 。
Mā ma zuì xǐ huan kàn jīng jù
My mother especially likes to watch Beijing opera.

126

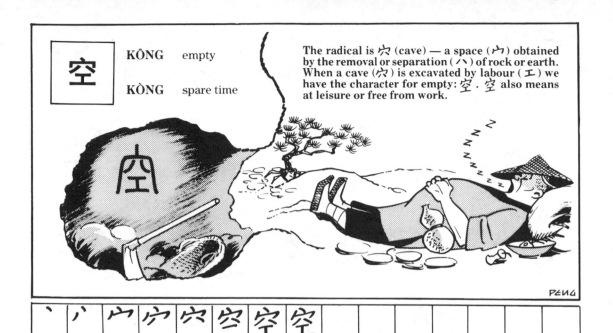

**空**

KŌNG    empty

KÒNG    spare time

The radical is 穴 (cave) — a space (宀) obtained by the removal or separation (八) of rock or earth. When a cave (穴) is excavated by labour (工) we have the character for empty: 空. 空 also means at leisure or free from work.

丶 丷 宀 宀 穴 空 空 空

| | | | |
|---|---|---|---|
| 空洞 | kōng dòng | cavity; empty | |
| 空防 | kōng fáng | air defence | |
| 空话 | kōng huà | empty talk; idle talk | |
| 空欢喜 | kōng huān xǐ | rejoice too soon | |
| 空间 | kōng jiān | space | |
| 空军 | kōng jūn | air force | |

| | | |
|---|---|---|
| 空阔 | kōng kuò | open; spacious |
| 空前绝后 | kōng qián jué hòu | unprecedented |
| 空头支票 | kōng tóu zhī piào | dud cheque |
| 空想 | kōng xiǎng | idle dream; fantasy |
| 空运 | kōng yùn | air transport; airlift |
| 空中 | kōng zhōng | in the sky; aerial; overhead |

*Example:*

别 空 想 了 ， 还 是 从 实 际 出 发 吧 。

Bié kōng xiǎng le   hái shì cóng shí jì chū fā ba

Stop daydreaming. Be realistic.

127

## 船

**CHUÁN**

boat; ship

As a memory aid, 船 could refer to a boat (舟) with eight (八) survivors or mouths (口) — an allusion to Noah's Ark. The radical 舟 is a picture of a boat. The phonetic 㕣 probably means a coast; so 船 is a coastal (沿) vessel (舟). No matter how useful such a vessel is, "Like a thread without a needle, a boat is useless without water."

丿 丿 刀 刀 舟 舟 舟' 舟㇏ 舟㇏ 船 船

| 船埠 | chuán bù | wharf; quay |
| 船壳 | chuán ké | hull |
| 船尾 | chuán wěi | stern |
| 船坞 | chuán wù | dock; shipyard |
| 船员 | chuán yuán | (ship's) crew |
| 船长 | chuán zhǎng | captain; skipper |
| 船只 | chuán zhī | shipping; vessels |

*Example:*

这 艘 船 的 船 员 们 都 很 勤 劳 。
Zhè sōu chuán de chuán yuán men dōu hěn qín láo
The sailors on this ship are hardworking.

128

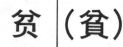

**贫（貧）**

PÍN    poor

The radical 貝, a picture of cowrie, shells once used as money, represents wealth. 分 is to divide or scatter. So 貧 is to squander (分) one's wealth (貝) — to be poor. Even the poor cannot afford to ignore the warning: "If the poor associates with the rich, he will soon have no trousers to wear."

| ノ | 八 | 分 | 分 | 分 | 分 | 贫 | 贫 | | | | | |
|---|---|---|---|---|---|---|---|---|---|---|---|---|

| 贫病交迫 | pín bìng jiāo pò | suffering from both poverty and sickness |
|---|---|---|
| 贫乏 | pín fá | poor; short; lacking |
| 贫寒 | pín hán | poor; poverty-stricken |
| 贫困 | pín kùn | poor; impoverished; in straitened circumstances |
| 贫民 | pín mín | poor people; pauper |
| 贫穷 | pín qióng | poor; needy; impoverished |
| 贫血 | pín xuè | anaemia |

*Example:*

在 他 贫 病 交 迫 的 时 候 ， 大 家 都 帮 助 他 。
Zài tā pín bìng jiāo pò de shí hou    dà jiā dōu bāng zhù tā
Everybody helped him out when he was sick and in poverty.

129

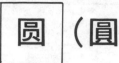

**YUÁN** round; dollar

This character for round or dollar has undergone many changes since its original form: ○. The ideograph 員, meaning round (○) like a cowrie (貝), soon replaced it. Then it was altered to 圓, being reclarified and surrounded by 囗. Although hollowed out to 圆, the dollar is still changeable; it's easier to change dollars into goods than goods into dollars!

PENG

丨 冂 冂 冃 冃 冃 圆 圆 圆 圆

| 圆规 | yuán guī | compasses |
| 圆滑 | yuán huá | smooth and evasive; slick and sly |
| 圆满 | yuán mǎn | satisfactory |
| 圆圈 | yuán quān | circle; ring |
| 圆舞曲 | yuán wǔ qǔ | waltz |
| 圆形 | yuán xíng | circular; round |
| 圆周 | yuán zhōu | circumference |
| 圆珠笔 | yuán zhū bǐ | ball-point pen; ball-pen |

*Example:*

问 题 圆 满 地 解 决 了 。
Wèn tí yuán mǎn de jiě jué le
The problem has been solved satisfactorily.

130

儿 （兒）

**ÉR** infant; child

儿 is a pictograph of the growing child — from the crawling infant with open fontanels (兒) to the little toddler (兒) with wobbly legs, now simplified to its present form: 儿. The loving care shown in the delineation of this character calls to mind the saying: "To understand your parents' love, raise your own children."

| 儿歌 | ér gē | children's song; nursery rhymes |
| 儿科 | ér kē | (department of) paediatrics |
| 儿女 | ér nǚ | sons and daughters; children |
| 儿孙 | ér sūn | children and grandchildren; descendants |
| 儿童 | ér tóng | children |

*Example:*

他 有 一 儿 一 女 。
Tā yǒu yī ér yī nǚ

He has a son and a daughter.

131

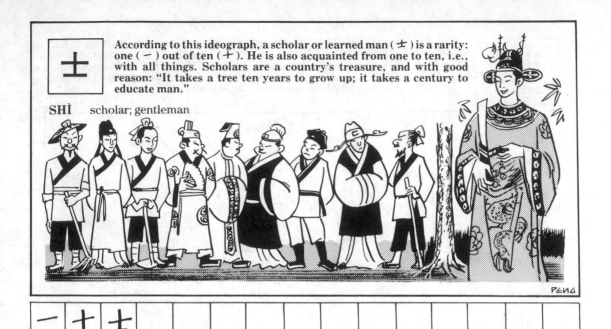

According to this ideograph, a scholar or learned man ( 士 ) is a rarity: one ( 一 ) out of ten ( 十 ). He is also acquainted from one to ten, i.e., with all things. Scholars are a country's treasure, and with good reason: "It takes a tree ten years to grow up; it takes a century to educate man."

**SHÌ**    scholar; gentleman

| 一 | 十 | 士 | | | | | | | | | | | |

| 士兵 | shì bīng | rank-and-file soldiers; privates |
| 士女 | shì nǚ | young men and women |
| 士气 | shì qì | morale |
| 士绅 | shì shēn | gentry |
| 士卒 | shì zú | soldiers; privates |

*Example:*

我 军 士 气 高 昂 。
Wǒ jūn shì qì gāo áng
Our army's morale is high.

132

## 做 ZUÒ

make; produce

做 sets forth man (亻) with a cause (故) to produce an effect. Hence the meaning: to make or produce. It also suggests man (亻) toiling (夊) until he gets old (古), sometimes for a fruitless cause. In the words of the proverb: "The hard work of a hundred years may be destroyed in an hour."

ノ 亻 仁 什 什 估 估 估 估 做 做

| 做东 | zuò dōng | play the host |
| 做法 | zuò fǎ | way of doing or making a thing |
| 做工 | zuò gōng | do manual work; work |
| 做鬼 | zuò guǐ | play tricks; play an underhand game |
| 做客 | zuò kè | be a guest |
| 做礼拜 | zuò lǐ bài | go to church; be at church |
| 做梦 | zuò mèng | have a dream; dream |
| 做贼心虚 | zuò zéi xīn xū | have a guilty conscience |

*Example:*

我 昨 天 到 一 个 老 朋 友 家 里 去 做 客 。
Wǒ zuó tiān dào yí ge lǎo péng you jiā lǐ qù zuò kè

I was a guest at an old friend's yesterday.

133

众 (衆)

**ZHÒNG** crowd; many

**The seal form 眾 shows three or many persons (人人人) as viewed by the eye (目). Modified to 眾, it was again altered to 众 — three persons, representing a crowd. It's easier to follow the crowd than to get the crowd to follow you. In the words of the proverb: "An army of a 1000 is easy to find; but, ah, how difficult to find a general!"**

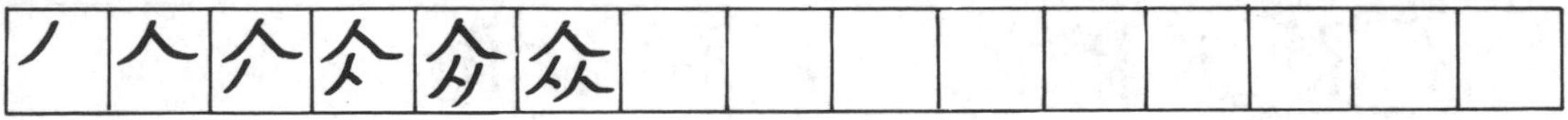

| | | | | | |
|---|---|---|---|---|---|
| 丿 | 人 | 亽 | 仌 | 众 | 众 |

| | | |
|---|---|---|
| 众多 | zhòng duō | multitudinous; numerous |
| 众口难调 | zhòng kǒu nán tiáo | it is difficult to cater for all tastes |
| 众口一词 | zhòng kǒu yī cí | with one voice; unanimously |
| 众目睽睽 | zhòng mù kuí kuí | the eyes of the masses are fixed on somebody or something |
| 众人 | zhòng rén | everybody |
| 众望 | zhòng wàng | people's expectations |

*Example:*

他 不 负 众 望 ， 得 到 冠 军 。

Tā bú fù zhòng wàng dé dào guàn jūn

He had come up to the people's expectations when he won the championship.

# 价 （價）

**JÌA**      price; value

The ideograph for price (價) is derived by putting 亻, man, the buyer against 賈, the seller. 賈, the seller, marks up the price to cover (西) his goods with value in cowries (貝). Paradoxically, the highest price you can pay for anything is to get it for nothing.

ノ 亻 亻 价 价 价

| 估价 | gū jià | estimate the value of; evaluate |
| 讲价 | jiǎng jià | bargain |
| 价格 | jià gé | price |
| 价目 | jià mù | marked price |
| 价值 | jià zhí | value; worth |
| 价值连城 | jià zhí lián chéng | worth several cities — invaluable; priceless |

*Example:*

这 些 资 料 对 我 们 很 有 价 值 。
Zhè xie zī liào duì wǒ men hěn yǒu jià zhí
This data is of great value to us

# 话 （話）

**HUÀ**  speech; words

話, meaning words or speech, is signified by words (言) of the tongue (舌).
講, meaning to speak or explain, is suggested by words (言) set in order (冓), 冓 being a graphic representation of the framework of a building. 講 is simplified to 讲. Sense is often linked with speech: "The full teapot makes no sound; the half-empty teapot makes much noise."

丶 讠 讠 讠 讠 讠 话 话

| | | | |
|---|---|---|---|
| 话别 | huà bié | say a few parting words; say good-bye |
| 话柄 | huà bǐng | subject for ridicule |
| 话旧 | huà jiù | talk over old times; reminisce |
| 话剧 | huà jù | modern drama; stage play |
| 话里有话 | huà lǐ yǒu huà | the words mean more than they say |
| 话题 | huà tí | subject of a talk; topic of conversation |
| 话筒 | huà tǒng | microphone; telephone transmitter; megaphone |
| 话头 | huà tóu | thread of discourse |

*Example:*

她 喜 欢 看 我 演 的 话 剧 。

Tā  xǐ  huan  kàn  wǒ  yǎn  de  huà  jù

She likes the plays that I perform in.

# 语（語）

**YǓ** language

吾, or five ( 五 ) mouths ( 口 ), stands for we, I, our or my. So our or my ( 吾 ) words ( 言 ) become language (語). Language is used in many ways. Some people use it to express thought, some to conceal thought, but most use it to replace thought.

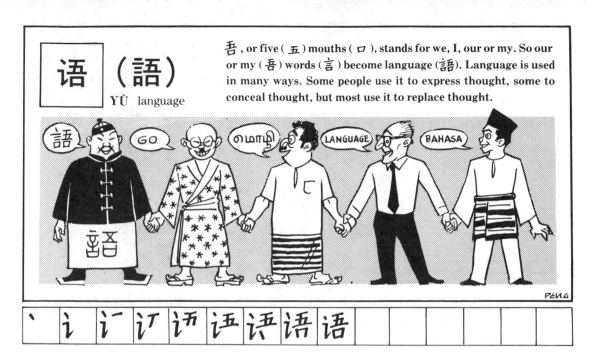

丶 讠 讠 订 讵 语 语 语 语

| | | | |
|---|---|---|---|
| 甜言蜜语 | tián yán mì yǔ | honeyed words | |
| 语词 | yǔ cí | words and phrases | |
| 语调 | yǔ diào | intonation | |
| 语法 | yǔ fǎ | grammar | |
| 语汇 | yǔ huì | vocabulary | |
| 语句 | yǔ jù | sentence | |

| | | |
|---|---|---|
| 语录 | yǔ lù | recorded utterance; quotation |
| 语气 | yǔ qì | tone; manner of speaking |
| 语无伦次 | yǔ wú lún cì | speak incoherently |
| 语言 | yǔ yán | language |
| 语音 | yǔ yīn | speech sounds; pronunciation |

*Example:*

她 的 语 音 好 。

Tā de yǔ yīn hǎo

She has good pronunciation.

## 去 QÙ

go; leave

去 is a pictograph of an empty vessel ( 厶 ) and its cover ( 土 ). The meaning "go" comes from the removal of the cover and contents of the vessel.

来 , meaning "come", is a pictograph of growing wheat or barley, gratefully acknowledged as having come from the heavens above.

PENG

一 十 土 去 去

| 去处 | qù chù | place to go; whereabouts |
| 去粗取精 | qù cū qǔ jīng | discard the dross and select the essential |
| 去垢剂 | qù gòu jì | detergent |
| 去路 | qù lù | the way along which one is going; outlet |
| 去年 | qù nián | last year |
| 去世 | qù shì | (of grown-up people) die; pass away |
| 去污粉 | qù wū fěn | household cleanser; cleanser |
| 去向 | qù xiàng | the direction in which somebody or something has gone |

*Example:*

有 谁 知 道 他 的 去 处 ?

Yǒu shuí zhī dao tā de qù chù

Who knows his where abouts?

138

**HUÍ** return

回 represents an eddy, like the curling clouds of smoke or whirlpools in water; or probably an object that rolls or turns on an axis; hence the idea of revolving or returning.

| 回避 | huí bì | evade; dodge |
| 回驳 | huí bó | refute |
| 回肠荡气 | huí cháng dàng qì | (of music, poems, etc.) soulstirring; heartrending |
| 回程 | huí chéng | return trip |
| 回答 | huí dá | answer; reply; response |
| 回顾 | huí gù | look back; review |

| 回击 | huí jī | return fire; counterattack |
| 回教 | Huí jiào | Islam |
| 回绝 | huí jué | decline, refuse |
| 回来 | huí lai | return; be back |
| 回头 | huí tóu | turn round; repent; later |
| 回想 | huí xiǎng | think back; recollect |

*Example:*

他 马 上 就 回 来 。

Tā mǎ shàng jiù huí lai

He'll be back in a minute.

139

凸, to protrude, is graphically represented by the shape of this character.

凹, a hollow or dent, is another primitive character clearly indicated by its shape.

**TŪ**

convex;
protruding

| | | | | |
|---|---|---|---|---|

| 凸版印刷 | tū bǎn yìn shuā | letterpress; relief or typographic printing |
|---|---|---|
| 凸窗 | tū chuāng | bay window |
| 凸轮 | tū lún | cam |
| 凸面镜 | tū miàn jìng | convex mirror |
| 凸透镜 | tū tòu jìng | convex lens |

| 凹版印刷 | āo bǎn yìn shuā | intaglio or gravure printing |
|---|---|---|
| 凹面镜 | āo miàn jìng | concave mirror |
| 凹透镜 | āo tòu jìng | concave lens |
| 凹凸印刷 | āo tū yìn shuā | embossing; die stamping |
| 凹陷 | āo xiàn | hollow; depressed |

*Example:*

这 条 路 凹 凸 不 平 。

Zhè  tiáo  lù  āo  tū  bù  píng

This road is full of bumps and holes.

# INDEX 附录

142

| | | | | | | | | | | |
|---|---|---|---|---|---|---|---|---|---|---|---|
| shū | 书 | 2:151 | tǔ | 土 | 1:81 | xiā | 虾 | 2:128 | yā | 鸭 | 2:96 |
| shǔ | 鼠 | 2:83 | | 吐 | 3:112 | | 瞎 | 3:93 | yà | 亚 | 2:3 |
| shuāng | 双 | 2:88 | tù | 兔 | 2:80 | xià | 下 | 1:37 | yán | 言 | 1:51 |
| shuǐ | 水 | 1:91 | | | | xiān | 仙 | 3:124 | | 炎 | 1:122 |
| shuì | 税 | 1:144 | | | | | 先 | 3:78 | | 岩 | 3:123 |
| | 睡 | 3:94 | wāi | 歪 | 2:101 | | 鲜 | 1:115 | yàn | 燕 | 2:99 |
| shuō | 说 | 1:64 | wài | 外 | 3:55 | xiàn | 线 | 2:135 | yáng | 羊 | 1:114 |
| sī | 丝 | 2:134 | wán | 完 | 2:34 | | 羡 | 1:120 | | 洋 | 1:119 |
| | 私 | 2:133 | wàn | 万 | 2:106 | | 现 | 3:4 | yào | 药 | 2:147 |
| | 思 | 3:97 | wáng | 王 | 3:1 | xiāng | 香 | 1:150 | yě | 也 | 1:45 |
| sū | 苏 | 1:146 | wǎng | 网 | 2:140 | xiǎng | 想 | 1:172 | yè | 叶 | 1:133 |
| suàn | 算 | 1:139 | wàng | 忘 | 1:174 | xiàng | 象 | 2:77 | | 夜 | 3:57 |
| suǒ | 所 | 2:19 | wéi | 维 | 2:144 | | 像 | 2:78 | yī | 衣 | 3:41 |
| | | | wèi | | | xiǎo | 小 | 1:19 | | 医 | 2:47 |
| tā | 他 | 1:46 | or wéi | 为 | 2:116 | xiào | 笑 | 1:140 | yǐ | 蚁 | 2:125 |
| tài | 太 | 1:17 | wěi | 尾 | 2:112 | xié | 协 | 3:74 | | 椅 | 3:86 |
| tān | 贪 | 2:9 | wèi | 未 | 1:168 | xiě | 写 | 2:149 | yì | 义 | 1:118 |
| tán | 谈 | 1:123 | | 胃 | 3:96 | xīn | 心 | 1:69 | | 忆 | 1:173 |
| téng | 疼 | 3:89 | wén | 闻 | 2:28 | | 新 | 2:24 | | 易 | 2:107 |
| tǐ | 体 | 1:163 | | 问 | 2:27 | xìn | 信 | 1:52 | | 逸 | 2:82 |
| tì | 剃 | 2:42 | wǒ | 我 | 1:43 | xíng | 行 | 3:62 | | 意 | 1:173 |
| tiān | 天 | 1:15 | wū | 乌 | 1:106 | xìng | 姓 | 1:85 | yīn | 因 | 2:4 |
| tián | 田 | 1:22 | | 屋 | 2:103 | xiōng | 兄 | 1:61 | yín | 银 | 2:11 |
| | 甜 | 3:103 | | | | | 凶 | 3:119 | yǐn | 引 | 2:39 |
| tīng | 听 | 3:105 | xī | 夕 | 3:51 | xióng | 熊 | 2:79 | | 饮 | 3:20 |
| tóu | 头 | 2:123 | | 西 | 1:35 | xiū | 休 | 1:33 | yìn | 印 | 2:150 |
| tū | 凸 | 3:140 | xí | 习 | 1:109 | xū | 须 | 2:122 | yīng | 英 | 1:136 |
| | 秃 | 1:145 | xǐ | 洗 | 3:79 | xué | 学 | 1:98 | yǒng | 永 | 1:92 |
| | 突 | 2:56 | | 喜 | 3:107 | xuě | 雪 | 2:148 | yǒu | 犹 | 2:58 |
| tú | 徒 | 3:65 | xì | 细 | 2:141 | xùn | 驯 | 2:67 | yǒu | 有 | 1:160 |